Girls Only?

BY THE SAME AUTHOR
*An Illustrated
Dictionary of Art Terms*

Girls Only?

GENDER AND POPULAR CHILDREN'S FICTION IN BRITAIN, 1880–1910

Kimberley Reynolds

*Lecturer at Ealing College of
Higher Education*

HARVESTER
WHEATSHEAF

New York   London   Toronto   Sydney   Tokyo   Singapore

First published 1990 by
Harvester Wheatsheaf,
66 Wood Lane End, Hemel Hempstead,
Hertfordshire, HP2 4RG
A division of
Simon & Schuster International Group

Printed and bound in Great Britain by
Billing and Sons Ltd, Worcester

British Library Cataloguing in Publication Data
Reynolds, Kimberley
    Girls only? : gender and popular children's
    fiction in Britain, 1880–1910.
    1. Sex roles. Influence of children's literature in
    English, 1880–1910
    I. Title
    305.2'3

ISBN 0–7108–1223–X

1 2 3 4 5   94 93 92 91 90

For my father:
RICHARD GRIFFITH

Contents

Illustrations

Illustrations within text

p. ii This featured story from 'Meadow-Sweet', the extra summer number of the *Girl's Own Paper* for 1891, encapsulates the feminine ideal: self-sacrifice, service, and piety.
p. 145 The new, more modern, mast-head for 1894.

Chapter opening pages

Chapter 1 From the *Girl's Own Annual* of 1890.
Chapter 2 Reproduced from the *Boy's Own Annual* of 1882.
Chapter 3 Reproduced from the *Boy's Own Annual* of 1882.
Chapter 4 Reproduced from the *Boy's Own Annual* of 1882.
Chapter 5 This cover for the 30 November 1889 number shows the *Girl's Own Paper*'s interest in cultivating girls' reading. The positive association between femininity and reading was frequently illustrated in late-Victorian/Edwardian novels and journals.
Chapter 6 From the *Girl's Own Annual* of 1890.

Plates

Plate 1 This illustration from Hesba Stretton's story of London slum life (*Little Meg's Children*, 1868) shows the ten-year-old heroine nursing her dying baby sister. One of the most popular of the evangelical books for children, Stretton's work combines graphic descriptions of the conditions of the poor with a sentimental portrayal of the redemptive powers of childhood innocence. This image of childhood is in marked contrast to earlier, more Calvinistic works such as Mrs Sherwood's *The*

Fairchild Family (1818), which were written to instruct sinful children in the need to turn to God.

Plate 2 This illustration from Evelyn Everett-Green's *A Wilful Maid* clearly shows the drive to reform those erring 'girls of the period'. From the fiercely independent and fashionable girl of the novel's opening, Lady Angela Goldhawk becomes a tearful and repentant young woman. At the book's conclusion she is happily married and, as her name had always foretold, soon to be the angel of her own household.

Plate 3 From Evelyn Everett-Green's *A Wilful Maid.*

Plate 4 'You are a wise maid to come to me to plead a wife's cause on behalf of an absent husband,' Queen Mary tells Lady Maud Melville. The three women in the picture, who are about to sort out the problems and misunderstandings made by bigoted and corrupt men, represent the myth of feminine power which provides self-esteem but depends on their not attempting to challenge the existing social order.

Plate 5 This illustration from L. T. Meade's *A Sweet Girl Graduate* shows the brilliant Miss Maggie Oliphant adopting a suitably demure pose beside Senior Wrangler Geoffrey Hammond. Not surprisingly, the two are married by the end of the novel, and Maggie (who received a First Class degree) leaves academia behind for a more fulfilling career as wife and mother.

Plate 6 'The Broken Contract' appeared in 'Snow-drops', the extra Christmas issue for 1885. The theme of the overworked seamstress is familiar in Victorian painting; here the paper's concern for such young women is made more poignant by the arrival of the two girls (typical *Girl's Own Paper* readers?) for whom the dresses were being made.

Plate 7 The April 1882 number of the *Girl's Own Paper* featured the North London Collegiate School for Girls. The illustration shows one of Miss Buss's 'gymnasium teas'. The contrast between the girls' dainty and restrained attitudes and the activities in which they are purportedly engaging seems to epitomise the contradictory nature of late-Victorian attitudes about what constituted a nice young lady.

Plate 8 Front cover, *Girl's Own Paper*, 19 October 1889.

Plate 9 From the *Girl's Own Paper*, 10 May 1890.

Plate 10 This featured illustration accompanied a one-column story about obedience and piety. The picture shows one of the dominant images of femininity of this period – the invalid mother looking into the distance (probably indicating approaching death).

Plate 11 The new, more manly, embrace is typified in this illustration to R. M. Ballantyne's *Twice Bought*, which was serialised in the *Boy's Own Annual* of 1883. Note the familiar mast-head with its many attributes illustrating typical male pursuits.

Plate 12 The *Boy's Own Paper* regularly ran 'how-to-make-it' features, such as this introduction to making a very complicated model steam engine which appeared in the 1889 annual.

Plate 13 Reproduced from the *Boy's Own Annual* of 1882.

Plate 14 This illustration, commissioned by the *Boy's Own Paper* and featured in the 29 December 1888 number, shows the paper's constant concern with promoting upright, courageous, Christian gentlemen. The nautical motif is equally characteristic.

Plate 15 This scene from Farrar's *Eric, or Little by Little* (1858) shows the wretched Eric at an early moment in his descent to depravity.

Plate 16 A typical selection of L. T. Meade's girls' stories. The rebellious heroines of the titles are inevitably tamed as their stories unfold.

Acknowledgements

I am grateful to many friends and colleagues at the University of Sussex who gave me their time and advice as this work evolved. Rachel Bowlby and Nicholas Tucker were closely involved in its preparation and gave me much good advice and support. Geoff Hemstedt read the manuscript at various stages and helped extensively in the final editing process. The library staff were indefatigable in tracking down out-of-print books and journals. I am especially grateful to Paul Yates, whose advice and encouragement have been invaluable throughout this project. Susanne Greenhalgh of the Roehampton Institute read my manuscript, as, of course, did my editor – Jackie Jones. To both of them I am in debt. Peter Reynolds has been tireless in his assistance. Without his help at home, at work, and on the wordprocessor(!) this book would never have been completed.

The author and publisher would also like to thank the Lutterworth Press for their permission to reproduce material from Wendy Forrester's *Great Grandmama's Weekly: A celebration of the Girl's Own Paper 1880–1901*.

Introduction

In reality every reader is, while he is reading, the reader of his own self. The writer's work is merely a kind of optical instrument which he offers to the reader to enable him to discern what, without this book, he would perhaps never have perceived for himself.

(Marcel Proust, *Time Regained*, Chapter 3)

Girls have always read more, and read more widely than boys. Although the social lives of many girls have been, and still are, more circumscribed than those of young men, their freedom to explore and experience a complex spectrum of literature, ranging from comics, fashion and beauty magazines, and romantic fantasies to works of recognised literary merit, far exceeds that of most boys and young men. Indeed, a substantial and profitable sector of the mass-circulation publishing market is directed specifically at female readers of all ages. Why are girls so generously catered for? In what ways do their adolescent reading habits affect their future reading habits? Why is it that boys either do not require, or find themselves refused, a similar literary range? What is the relationship between notions of sexual difference inscribed in juvenile fiction generally, and its sectors directed at young readers of different sexes? How is this related to social practice? These and many other questions arise when juvenile and popular fiction, and the nature of sexual difference, are examined in parallel.

The phenomenon which is juvenile fiction can largely be viewed as originating in Britain in the 1880s. The publication of children's books and periodicals of late-Victorian and Edwardian England was essentially a new enterprise, arising in tandem with the educational reforms of 1870 and 1880, and the advent of new printing technology which made it possible to produce cheap books and periodicals on a large scale. The arrival of the enormously popular *Boy's Own Paper* and *Girl's Own Paper*, in 1879 and 1880 respectively, can be regarded as confirmation of an established mass audience for juvenile publishing, and it is with the period between 1880–1910 that I am particularly concerned. In order to understand this period, it is necessary to know something about changes in attitude to childhood and the young reader which took place earlier in the century. Chapter 1 outlines these and also explores the dialectical relationship between juvenile publishing and the expansion of education. In particular, it looks at the ways in which separate literatures and syllabuses were designed and assigned according to class and sex.

Studying the creation of the niche inserted into the established publishing world by the new, popular, juvenile fiction – its manufacture, objectives, and commercial responses – offers many insights into the forms and motivations of present-day children's books, and in particular the images of masculinity and femininity which tend to be reflected in today's juvenile fiction. Of key interest is the fact that then as now there existed a crude split between what can be designated 'high' and 'low' areas of juvenile publishing. Such divisions tend to be significant pointers to prevailing attitudes towards class and gender. High fiction consists of those works recognised as having literary merit, among which boys' adventure and school stories, depictions of bourgeois family life, and a hybrid of fantasy and riddle à la *Alice in Wonderland* or Lear's 'nonsense' books predominate. Low fiction includes those works denied any literary merit, notably girls' stories and 'bloods' or comics. The high, which also contains the mainstream of children's literature, tended to be read by both sexes. It glorified the child, and made links between a notion of moral order and the child's capacity to use language 'purely': that is without the ambiguities, double meanings, and compromises characteristic of adult communication. In these works, knowledge is power, and for the most part possessed by educated, male children of the middle and upper classes. The low-status or mass-circulation books and periodicals, by contrast, were predominantly written for girls and working-class children, and appear to have been as much concerned with sensationalism as with didacticism.

In his survey of *The English Common Reader* (1957), Richard Altick describes the anxiety surrounding popular fiction which developed during the latter half of the nineteenth century. This anxiety originated from the belief that entertaining reading matter would stimulate the working classes to read, and thereby develop the potential for radicalism and rebellion. It was also feared that reading would promote social degeneracy of a different kind by catering to a class historically unaccustomed to reading, and therefore believed to lack the necessary mechanisms of taste and appetite control. Instead of the well-regulated reading habits that Altick associates with a typical classical education of the day (deemed by many to be anti-intellectual and determined to destroy any natural appreciation of literature through insistence on literality and grammar), a hunger for escapist venues was being fed by publishers who recognised the potential profitability of a market comprised of entertaining, sensational fiction. Libraries, where up to 90 per cent of books circulated were classified as fiction,[1] began to be likened by some to pubs, and it was suggested that once embarked on a course of novel reading, boys were unlikely ever to make much progress in later life.[2] One correspondent to the *Evening Standard* (January 1891) reported that nine out of ten chairs in his local library were filled by 'loafing office boys or clerks. . . using their masters' time for devouring all the most trivial literary trash', while employers complained publicly that the advent of the penny-dreadful made it impossible to get work out of office boys and errand runners.[3] Thus an economic argument was added to support the class-based objection to boys' reading popular fiction. Not necessarily a new complaint, this prejudice against boys imbibing light fiction reached a crescendo in the closing years of the century.

While the division of boys' fiction into 'high' and 'low' mainly reflected the class of those for whom it was intended, most fiction specifically written for and read by girls was categorised as low regardless of the class of the audience. Class, however, was part of the argument upon which fiction written for girls was dismissed, as were economic considerations. This can be seen clearly in Edward J. Salmon's survey 'What girls read' (*Nineteenth Century*, October 1886) which describes the effect of the penny novelette on working-class girls. The injury done to boys by the penny-dreadful, he suggests, is as nothing when compared to that caused by the equally 'low and vicious' character of their sisters' fiction, the action of which was 'more invidious and subtle' for being almost exclusively domestic. Salmon's charge that sensational fiction promoted unsuitable fantasies which unfitted girls for domestic duties and made them dissatisfied with manual labour is representative of the attack against the bottom end of mass-produced fiction for girls at this time.

Fiction for middle-class girls, by contrast, was seized upon as having a potentially beneficial function: that of keeping young ladies pure by deflecting them from inappropriate reading matter and the knowledge of the world it might impart. Such knowledge would render them unfit for a marriage market that demanded docile, domestic angels. Apart from this, those stories written specifically for middle-class girls rather than as family fiction appear to have had no literary status or credibility. I have looked at a selection of such works to try to see how far this harsh judgement was an accurate assessment of their authors' skills, and to what extent publishers' dictates and a general prejudice based on male educational superiority may be claimed to have distorted their reception. Reason suggests that at least a proportion of the massive amount of fiction produced for middle-class girls during this period is due for critical reappraisal; especially as some of the most prominent writers of girls' stories also wrote historical and biblical works read by children of both sexes. Whatever the reason, such stories were highly popular with parents, publishers, and girl readers alike, appearing in 'shoals' annually.[4] By 1884, the *Girl's Own Paper*, with its combination of light fiction and domestic hints, was reputed to have achieved the highest circulation of any English illustrated magazine.[5]

The debate over what constituted appropriate reading matter was a significant public preoccupation, as evidenced by the variety and number of articles and publications to which it gave rise. Newspapers and periodicals carried articles on the effect of different sorts of reading matter on both boys and girls, on the use, development, and suitability of free libraries and their contents, on the relationship between the degeneracy of language, the institution of universal, compulsory education and the phenomenon of popular fiction and offered advice on what books to lend and give. The bulk of these pieces centre around anxiety over what girls read, and Chapters 4 and 5 examine the social and ideological reasons for this emphasis. One factor is certain: girls' stories in themselves were not and are not sufficient, and while girls have read and still do read them in vast numbers, they have always supplemented their literary diet. In the nineteenth century their reading would probably also have included what Ruskin described as 'every fresh addition to the fountain of folly' (the three-volume novels which made up the bulk of the lending libraries' stock), and works from the high sector of juvenile publishing. Among these would have been books and periodicals directed at their brothers. Contemporary articles, autobiographies, and surveys testify to the eclectic nature of girls' reading by the latter half of the century. One of the central concerns of this book has therefore been to consider why the sub-genre, girls' fiction, developed, what it was intended to do, and in what ways it may both have catered for and failed to satisfy the demands of its readership. At the same time, it questions the nature and function of juvenile fiction for boys, not simply to see what it provided which was not contained in fiction for girls, but also with a view to understanding why a similarly exclusive, seductive, and substantial sub-genre did not develop for boys, and the implications of this gap.

Locating this discussion in late-Victorian and Edwardian England automatically places it in a context of change and resulting anxiety about change. It is necessary therefore to relate the strongly conservative drive characteristic of girls' stories to a collective psychological need for cultural synthesis in an age of transition, and to see it as part of a reaction against public expressions of instability. Equally significant in fiction for boys is the handling and depiction of women, who were traditionally regarded as the safe houses for and transmitters of culture. The concept of adolescence was developed in the nineteenth century, and it seems that juvenile publishing as a whole responded to the newly-emphasised period of transition between childhood and adulthood in part because it provided a metaphor for the time.

Girls Only? came about through my reading of a large body of popular nineteenth-century juvenile fiction in the light of contemporary critical theory. While the social, historical and economic conditions out of which these works arose feature largely, my central interest was to understand the cultural significance of boys' and girls' reading habits. Using essentially psychoanalytic, feminist, and structuralist approaches, I have tried to explain the difference in kind and quantity between girls' and boys' reading matter and, especially, why it is that girls can and do read across the spectrum of juvenile fiction, while boys have never readily admitted to reading, or desiring to read, works directed at their female cohort. While debate has traditionally been concerned with what girls read, boys' reading has always been more restricted. Chapters 2 and 4 consider some of the possible consequences of this for gender-development, and specifically question the prevailing theory that girls are provided with their own literature to compensate them for a need which is not met socially or in mainstream children's fiction, while boys find their diet satisfactory. This is an oversimplification which both fails to take adequate account of the derisory attitude to girls' fiction and the repercussions of this on the texts and their readers, and also ignores the restrictions surrounding boys' reading. Developing this line of thought, these chapters explore the different goals of books directed specifically at boys and girls and their likely effects on the young reader's attitude towards his/her sexuality.

Finally, I have been interested in seeing if there is a 'right' reading codified within children's fiction of this period (based on what is said, how it is received within the text, and how works are resolved), and if so, whether or not this has potentially different implications for readers of different sex. Ultimately, any reader, male or female, adult or child, is the subject of his/her own text when reading, and is responding to cultural cues and signals to which s/he is already conditioned. What *Girls Only?* seeks to explain on the basis of fiction written during the formative years of juvenile publishing, is the way in which children learn to perceive themselves and their cultural roles through the fiction written and marketed for them, and the likely implications of reading on the acquisition of sexual identity.

Chapter 1

'Look into their books': social attitudes to children's reading and the impact of compulsory education

Children's literature and reading before 1880

The single most important factor in the burgeoning of juvenile fiction has to do with the changing attitudes of commercial publishers as they became aware of the existence of a readership to which they had hitherto singularly failed to address themselves. Although since the end of the eighteenth century a small number of books had been produced specifically for children, the vast majority of such works were less concerned with catering to the needs and tastes of their young audience than with providing instruction and offering examples to follow.

Publishers of children's books in the first half of the century tended to be less interested in profit than in inculcating specific religious, social and ideological precepts; they subscribed to the prevailing idea that the child was born sinful and needed to be catechised into repentance and piety and the pieces they published were intensely didactic. Nor did they make concessions to the child's vocabulary or imaginative needs. Opportunity for imparting knowledge in the form of facts – biological, biblical, zoological, geographical, or historical – was rarely missed. While we must allow for the fact that perceptions of what constituted an interesting and pleasurable read have changed radically over the past 100 to 150 years, it is reasonable to assume that lessons such as those contained in Mrs Sherwood's *History of the Fairchild Family* (1818) must frequently have preyed on the minds of young readers. For instance, the gruesome fate of the naughty child who was burned to death (all because her parents failed sufficiently to chastise her) alternating with verbose and pedantic discussions of theology seem to modern eyes to offer a far from satisfactory literary encounter for the new young reader.

There are several factors which contributed to this attitude towards children and their literature. Many of these have been fully explored by a number of historians of children's literature.[1] What has not been considered is the relationship between the recognition of the child as a potential consumer and the education policies of the second half of the last century. These are significant because together they provided access to the ideas, vocabulary, and behavioural models which helped the child to define himself/herself socially. The idea of the child reader as consumer grew gradually throughout the nineteenth century. Its evolution can be seen clearly in the records of the two largest evangelical publishing houses, the Religious Tract Society (RTS) and the Society for Promoting Christian Knowledge (SPCK). Their records suggest that much of the initial resistance to recognising children as potential purchasers of books was bound up with the widespread reluctance to promote universal literacy which prevailed for much of the century. George III had given expression to popular feeling when he declared that it was his wish 'that every poor child in my dominions should be taught to read the Bible'.[2] Early organised literacy programmes were designed to achieve just that – to provide sufficient reading skills to allow the mass of the population to spell out the Bible and other suitable pieces distributed by the Church. It was believed that establishing basic literacy would improve the work-force, which could be given simple written instructions for operating machinery and for following the wishes of its masters. Both the ability to read approved religious matter and information related to work called for *limited* literacy only and depended on restricting new readers' contact to reading matter which could improve and instruct. The prospect of a newly-literate population coming into contact with works which had the potential to disrupt, corrupt, or incite dissatisfaction was anathema.[3]

Those against reading feared for the safety of the existing social structure if the hitherto uneducated mass of the population were to come into contact with revolutionary ideas which they were unprepared to resist. There was also anxiety about the moral consequences of reading fiction and the possible repercussions for industry if the working classes became seduced by reading so that it hindered their ability to work. However, it soon became evident that once reading skills were acquired they were rarely used exclusively, or even predominantly, for ingesting the good works which were so vigorously distributed in the form of tracts, mottoes, calendars, pamphlets, and reward books.[4] New readers of every age were attracted to the cheap and bawdy chapbooks, thrillers, and comics which became increasingly plentiful as the century progressed.

The evangelical publishing houses soon recognised the need to counter the attractions of cheap, sensational and potentially damaging publications with lively and appealing works of their own. Still deeply concerned with forging an alliance between literacy and morality, they accepted that entertainment was a necessary sauce to aid in the digestion of the religious and social convictions which were the principal ingredients of their publications. They soon discovered that a large and enthusiastic audience existed once it was suitably catered for. Although initially surprised at the financial success of their more liberal editorial policies, the RTS and SPCK quickly accommodated themselves to the notion that sugaring the Christian message was the way to ensure cash injections for other branches of their work. With the advantage of hindsight, it is now possible to see how the initial impetus to secure a larger audience became the thin end of the wedge of the commercialism which was to dominate juvenile publishing by the end of the century. Though initially intending only to make their publications more appealing to young readers in order to lure them away from chapbooks and other unsuitable publications, publishers soon discovered the enormous financial possibilities offered by the new readership. In 1831 the SPCK formed its Committee of General Literature and Education; from the time of its inception until roughly the First World War, this, together with the revamped Tract Committee, proved the Society's greatest single area of profit.

By 1869 the SPCK was competing successfully against those publications which it held were 'openly addressed to the passions and prejudices of the Multitude . . . encouraging ribaldry, sedition and hostility to the established Church.'[5] The statement of the Committee of General Literature and Education in the annual report of 1870–71 celebrates this fact, and the language and tone used clearly indicate the Committee's increasing interest in commercial rather than strictly religious success.

4

Approval of the *secular* literature published of late by the Committee has been widely and honestly accorded. The 'get-up' of the books has been made as attractive as possible without increasing the price. . . . Boys and girls will turn eagerly to such capital stories as 'Esperance', 'Nobody's Child', 'Silent Jim', 'Sunshine Bill', 'Big Bruce', 'Five Pounds' Reward', 'Life in the Walls', Mrs Carey Brock's 'Clear Shining After Rain', and 'Hatty and Nellie', 'Ruth Lee', and 'Marion'.[6]

The RTS shared this attitude and, after an ebullient first year of publishing the *Girl's Own Paper*, noted in the annual report for 1880–81: 'Some of the Society's friends have complained of the *Boy's Own Paper* and *Girl's Own Paper* as being too secular in tone,' but roundly rejected such criticism on the grounds that, 'the attempt to give them an exclusively religious character would be to defeat the very purpose for which they were intended.'[7] By 1880 commercial success had led even the most committed Christian publishers to reduce religious content, increase the number of entertaining features, and establish the practice of producing publications directed specifically at boys or girls rather than at young readers generally.

Compulsory education and the social meaning of literacy

Historians of children's literature generally agree that the decade between the 1870 Education Act and the introduction of compulsory education in 1880 saw the rapid expansion of that branch of the publishing industry directed at young readers. Once the scale of the audience was established, a new breed of publisher set out to commandeer the juvenile market with alacrity. No longer were the RTS and the SPCK undisputed rulers over the magic kingdom of children's fiction. Their supremacy was successfully challenged by such adventurous publishers as the Chambers brothers and John Cassell. Using new publishing methods, advertising, marketing, and generally modernising their approaches, these entrepreneurs rapidly created and catered for a new market of 'colossal dimensions'.[8]

Soon the firm founded by Cassell was claiming that it could 'quote the current official figure of elementary school children as the Cassell constituency'.[9]

The speed with which a vast range of high-quality books for children was written and produced is impressive. By the 1880s the range of fictional books alone included adventure stories, historical fiction, school stories, and domestic stories, and numbered among its writers for boys such distinguished figures as R. M. Ballantyne, H. Rider Haggard, Captain Marryat, Mayne Reid, R. L. Stevenson, G. A. Henty, F. Anstey, Frederick Farrar, Thomas Hughes and Talbot Baines Reed. Among those producing books for girls by this time were Mrs Ewing, Anne Beale, L. T. Meade, Anna Sewell and Charlotte M. Yonge.[10] Not all of these writers or their works were new, but through cheap reprints, lending libraries and periodical serialisation their works became accessible to the masses, making it possible to see the commercial and ideological potential of juvenile fiction as popular entertainment. Also by this time, as indicated by designations in increasingly detailed and elaborate catalogues and in the recommendations of critics, it is possible to see the emerging demarcation between books aimed at young readers of different sexes, which I perceive to be instrumental in forging attitudes towards and establishing distinct 'high' and 'low' areas of juvenile publishing. So-called high works were those credited with literary merit and low works were those deemed at best frivolous and at worst unwholesome or decadent. As will become apparent, these divisions correspond in many ways to emphases in the new Board of Education schools.

Disquiet about universal literacy did not simply disappear with the advent of compulsory education. There remained, especially in the established press, vociferous opposition to the 'gutter press' and sensational fiction. However, by 1880 the debate about whether or not all the poor should be taught to read and associated anxieties about *what* should be read are both residual discourses which actually obscure the emerging policy of encouraging the printing, distribution, and consumption of entertaining fiction. Why this is so and how it relates to the development of fiction for children will become clear when changes in attitude and practice regarding the teaching of literacy and the publishing of material for new readers are examined. What becomes evident is that the encouragement and acceptance of reading for pleasure is in marked contrast to attitudes towards any kind of reading outside the pages of the Bible so much in evidence in the first fifty years and more of the century.

This change came about through a slippage which occurred around the issues of literacy and education. This involved first accepting the existence of a literate working class, then broadening toleration for what was read until reading *of a particular kind* came to be seen as a desirable leisure activity for 'the lower orders'. One key factor in effecting this slippage relates to what appears to have been the regular tendency for most of the century to underestimate the numbers of the poor who were literate. This was due in some measure to the problematic nature of the evidence and the unstable meaning of the term 'literate' itself. I use the term 'literate' to mean the ability to read simple but unfamiliar pieces of writing unassisted. Whatever the exact part-of-population which could by this definition be considered literate, it is clear that it had been increasing steadily long before the advent of compulsory education.[11]

Contemporary journals provide ample evidence to suggest that working-class literacy was well established and at some levels or for some purposes recognised to be so prior to 1870. This passage from an 1838 number of the *Servant's Magazine* (1837–6) is an example:

> Times have changed since the great bulk of female servants were unable to read. . . . Servants are now fond of reading, and this is well; but it is of vast importance that what they read should be adapted to promote their true welfare, to render them more useful in their station, more contented with the arrangements of a kind Providence, which have placed them in it, and more alive to the hallowed principles which can alone prepare them for the engagements and the happiness of heaven.[12]

A later article, 'The byways of literature: reading for the

million' (*Blackwoods Magazine*, August 1858), set out the problems occasioned by a literate working class which, the piece implied, was unable to resist the enticements of the abundant cheap papers, periodicals, and other forms of writing suddenly available to it. Significantly, the focus of anxiety in the *Blackwoods* article is not *whether* the working class could read, but *what* it read: 'Let us give the masses all credit for their gift of reading; but before we glorify ourselves over the march of intelligence, let us pause first to look into their books.'[13] Thus, while the piece anticipates the general acceptance or recognition of a literate working class, it continues to express anxiety over reading for pleasure. Unless the poor were reading material designed to instruct them in conduct or to improve technological skills, reading often continued to be regarded as a suspect activity.

It was this attitude which led to the failure of Samuel Whitbread's Parochial Schools Bill (1807). During the Parliamentary debate, MPs objected to Whitbread's proposal to provide education for the working class out of the public purse on the grounds that

> it would, in effect, be found to be prejudicial to their morals and happiness; it would teach them to despise their lot in life, instead of making them good servants in agriculture, and other laborious employments to which their rank in society had destined them; instead of teaching them subordination, it would render them factious and refractory, as was evident in the manufacturing counties; it would enable them to read seditious pamphlets, vicious books, and publications against Christianity; it would render them insolent to their superiors; and, in a few years, the result would be, that the legislature would find it necessary to direct the strong arm of power towards them, and to furnish the executive magistrates with much more vigorous laws than were now in force.[14]

By mid-century such arguments were becoming unfashionable, and opponents of increased literacy were rapidly becoming outnumbered by those who, like Samuel Smiles, believed that the real danger is in excess of ignorance, not in excess of knowledge; in the blind groping in the darkness, and not in the light which illuminates every nook and cranny of the social edifice.[15]

Herein lies a crucial point: education was coming to be seen as instrumental in containing the threat posed by a literate working class. In other words, education (as opposed to simple literacy) began to be considered an effective means of social control and a way of maintaining the status quo at a time when many social and economic factors had undergone radical change.[16] It seems likely that a fear about a newly literate working class when there already was one was an attempt to contain any potential challenge it presented, partially through unconscious repression, but also in part through deliberate policy. Once education began to be perceived as the solution to the problem, the idea of a working class which could read was no longer something to be feared, but became something to be worked for. It is not coincidental that these changes in attitude towards education and literacy took place in tandem with reforms in the child-labour laws which released large numbers of children from the burdens of wage earning. It seems that these two factors (that education could be used to support the existing social structure and to look after the children and young people who had been legislated on to the streets) resulted in the setting up of a system of education not primarily designed to spread literacy or train pupils to think, but to look after and train children to become model members of the working class.

It was necessary that the government take control of this operation because, as John Stuart Mill had made clear in his *Principles of Political Economy* (1848), the existing system whereby the middle and upper classes used unofficial measures such as voluntary education establishments and the distribution of religious and moral tracts to instruct the working class was no longer effective. Mill's analysis establishes parallels between this failure and the independent existence of a literate working class.

The working-classes have taken their interests into their own hands, and are perpetually showing that they think the interests of

9

their employers not identical with their own, but opposite to them. Some among the higher classes flatter themselves that these tendencies may be counteracted by moral and religious education, but they have let the time go by for giving an education which can serve their purpose. The principles of the Reformation have reached as low down in society as reading and writing, and the poor will no longer accept morals and religion of other peoples' prescribing.[17]

At roughly the same time that Mill was writing, the government, which in the early years of the century had been content to leave education to the care of voluntary organisations' Sunday and day schools or the working class's own dame and evening classes, felt compelled to take an active part in its organisation.[18] It was with state intervention, first in the form of grants and the appointment of inspectors who ensured they were properly spent, and culminating in the Education Acts of 1870 and 1880, that significant changes in the aims of educationalists became apparent. These have a direct bearing on the establishing of reading habits and on the solidification of gender divisions as we know them today and as they are reflected in fiction for the young. Before considering these issues, it is necessary to consider why they evolved; why education took the turn that it did. When the existing provision of schooling and the orthodoxy surrounding it are examined, it becomes apparent that the social meaning of literacy changed significantly along with educational policy.

Much of the hostility that the upper and middle classes felt towards the idea of a literate working class arose from the fear that the existing relations between the classes would not be able to be maintained. Because an education had long been a kind of social *passe-partout*, it was necessary to devise a system which would make it possible for there to be universal experience of school without taking away a principal source for the legitimation of the status of those in power. The education given to the working classes, therefore, could not be the same as that received by the upper classes. Until this could be ensured, a strong conservative faction, which opposed the spread of literacy principally on moral grounds, continued to exist.

The educational reforms which took place in the closing decades of the last century undoubtedly laid the foundations for a national system of education and paved the way for the development of higher education. Nevertheless, it is important to note that widespread literacy in the poor sector of the population had existed *prior* to the advent of universal, compulsory education and to recognise that with state intervention in the organisation of schooling, the perceptions and goals of education were changed so that they replicated and underpinned the existing hegemonic structure. A consequence of this was that attitudes towards reading of all kinds were substantially altered; this in turn had extensive and lasting repercussions on publishing in general and the development of juvenile fiction in particular.

The attitudes and conclusions contained in such instrumental documents as the report of the Statistical Society, which in 1830 investigated the state of schooling, are revealing. This provides emotional accounts of the conditions in which the working classes received their schooling, and criticised what passed for education on the grounds that it was not what the poor needed to know. The following summary of dame schools in Manchester is typical:

DAME SCHOOLS

Under this head are included all those schools in which reading only, and a little sewing, are taught. This is the most numerous class of schools, and they are generally in the most deplorable condition. The greater part of them are kept by females, but some by old men, whose only qualification for this employment seems to be their unfitness for every other. Many . . . are engaged at the same time in some other employment, such as shopkeeping, sewing, washing, etc. which renders any regular instruction among their scholars absolutely impossible. Indeed, neither parents nor teachers seem to consider this as the principal objective in sending their children to these schools, but generally say that they go in order to be taken care of and out of the way at home.[19]

The same report, however, adds a footnote indicating that there was widespread resistance on the part of parents to the new infant schools on the grounds that the children *'learn nothing'* [my italics] there. It seems likely that there were disparate notions of what schooling should offer children, or at least what it should appropriately offer the children of the poor. The working-class appeared anxious to learn to read, seeing this as the key to all educational (and possibly social) doors, while their social superiors believed that school should teach values and behaviour.[20]

This would account for the widespread belief that existing working-class schools were ineffective. Because conditions were poor and the education 'inappropriate', such schools were presented by the middle class as virtually valueless. Dickens, for example, caricatured them as establishments where, 'in a purblind, groping way', pupils learnt 'to read, write and cipher on the very smallest scale'.[21] The reality was somewhat different. Compare this essentially bourgeois perception of dame-school education with the description of Charles Shaw of Tunstall (born 1832) who actually attended such an establishment, Old Betty W's school:

> The course of education given by the old lady was very simple, and graded with almost scientific precision. There was an alphabet, with rude pictures, for beginners . . . though she never taught writing, her scholars were generally noted for their ability to read while very young. I know I could read my Bible with remarkable ease when I left her school, when seven years old.
>
> Betty's next grade, after the alphabet, was the reading-made-easy book. . . . The next stage was spelling and reading of the Bible. For those successful in these higher stages, old Betty had peculiar honours (carrying ashes to the ash-heap, sitting on the highest chair in the cottage). . . . There was yet another distinction the old lady had to bestow. She taught both boys and girls who were successful in reading how to knit stockings. She was a remarkable knitter herself, and could carry on this occupation with the regularity almost of a machine, while her eyes were everywhere in her school. I knew boys who knitted stockings for their families. They thus learnt reading and knitting, instead of reading and writing.[22]

Most of those who attended dame schools, both good and bad, did acquire basic literacy, and some became proficient at and enjoyed reading, though for full-time wage earners there was likely to be little time to indulge this pastime. Why was it that the full extent of working-class literacy was never acknowledged and that working-class schools were considered by middle-class authorities to be 'unsuitable'? The Statistical Society report, for instance, criticised the dame and day schools its compilers visited for failing to provide 'a really useful education', by which was meant one emphasising the skills and behaviour deemed desirable in a working class. It seems likely that this refusal to accept that there existed an effective educational tradition among the poor was at least in part grounded in fear. As long as literacy was the fulcrum of education, possessing it necessarily put the lower classes on an educational par with their social betters.[23]

For Lévi-Strauss, 'the struggle against illiteracy is indistinguishable, at times, from the increased power exerted over the individual citizen by the central authority.'[24] When the nineteenth-century educationalists championed the cause of literacy as a social crusade, this surely lay at the back of the campaign. In a technological and increasingly bureaucratic age, a truly illiterate working class was inconceivable; a working class which could both read and write and viewed these skills as the same as those exercised by their betters was too threatening. It was therefore necessary to provide schooling which would teach sufficient skill in reading and writing to meet the demands of a modern workforce while simultaneously ensuring that these attainments did not match those acquired by the educated élite. In the Board of Education schools, therefore, each social category had its own provision and place. Working-class pupils were given a curriculum which attempted to instil habits of obedience and frugality but insufficient knowledge of political economy to enable them to interfere in the decision-making of their masters. Middle-class pupils, too, were provided with a utilitarian style of education, emphasising skills such as accountancy, which would be required by small businessmen. The upper classes, by contrast, received a largely classical education.[25] The members of the Taunton Commission (1868) wryly noted the impetus and effect of this stratified system of education and the increased significance of the now prolonged and esoteric schooling given to upper-class children. The classics were, they observed, valued 'for their own sake, and perhaps even more for the value at present assigned to them in English society. They [professional men and lesser gentry] have nothing to look to but education to keep their sons on a high social scale.'[26]

The effect of this stratified system of education was to emphasise the difference between the language used by the upper classes and that used by the lower classes. Thus, even though it was now accepted that the working classes could read and write, they were not deemed able to comprehend or appreciate 'literature'. Recent research into nineteenth-century schooling suggests that this was not merely a trick of perception, but a fact: there was an actual *decline* in the teaching of reading and writing which was directly linked to the exodus of children from full-time work and the introduction of compulsory school attendance.[27]

Whether or not this is true, the *belief* that there was a decline in standards is significant for it reflects recognition that there was a difference in status between what was read by the poor and what was read by their social superiors. These differences in status had always existed, but at this period became entrenched. The government lifted the heavy duties which had kept prices up making it legally possible to provide the large numbers of low-status periodicals, papers and stories which the basic working-class education fitted its recipients to read and enjoy. Thus children coming through the state system were able to satisfy their taste for reading the easy and entertaining new material now available and which, 'by no stretch of the imagination could be called literary'.[28] Reading for pleasure was no longer perceived to be a threatening activity as long as what was read was appropriate to the class (or sex) of the reader. The element of entertainment therefore became a distinguishing characteristic of low-status publications.

Curriculum: sex, class and the classics

We are living in an age which professes to educate the poor and fit them for a higher life, and open to them the prizes once confined to the richer classes; and yet we find that the race for distinctions is after all practically confined to the rich, and that the poor have been gulled out of their expected privileges.

(J. P. Mahaffy, 'Modern education', 1897)

Thus far I have talked about some of the changes which took place in the latter half of the nineteenth century and the growth of the perception of the child reader (as opposed to the larger category of new readers) as consumer. This perception generated new ideas about the content and presentation of books for children. The result was that children's literature rapidly became one of the largest sections on publishers' lists. However, I have also emphasised that there were significant social constructions attached to literacy and that these were mirrored in the educational reforms of the late-nineteenth century. Together they attempted to make a distinction between the working class's ability to read and the familiarity with literature and literary language which came about through the extended education received by their social betters. The result of this effort was to designate children's literature as pre-literary. It quickly came to be associated with popular culture and uncanonised writing.[29]

The tendency to regard much children's literature as belonging to the low-status areas of publishing was well established by the end of the last century as can be seen in the efforts made to combat this prejudice by those authors and critics concerned with bringing children's literature before the public as a genre in its own right.[30] It is now time to examine the ways in which this classification came about, and how it was related to prevailing attitudes to class and gender in the newly compulsory education system.

CLASS

Once a three-tier school system had been established, the goal of which was to turn out 'the Briton who will be one of the *muscular workers* . . . the Briton whose work requires knowledge of the modern world . . . [and] the Briton who is to be a *leader* . . .'[31], the repercussions were manifold. Those repercussions with a direct bearing on the development of juvenile publishing and its impact on gender and class roles centre on the teaching of English.

Initially, each class of student received instruction in English only as part of his/her lessons in reading and writing (English as a subject in its own right did not exist until the turn of the century).[32] Teachers employed techniques derived from the teaching of the classics to instruct their pupils in the basic principles of the orthography, etymology, syntax, and grammar of standard English.

Although the recognised pinnacle of linguistic achievement was the same for all students, not all were expected to achieve it. The muscular, modern, and leading Briton were scheduled to leave school at ages 14, 16, and 18 respectively,[33] and it is in the leaving age that the underlying determination to provide different educations for different classes is most clearly manifested. Thus, though at the primary level the subjects taught to each class of student might be roughly similar, they were taught to different ends, determined by whether or not the pupil was intended to go on to higher rungs on the educational ladder; a decision which was largely determined by class.

The class-based nature of education at this time is underlined by persistent opposition throughout the century to funding for higher education coming out of the public purse (and thereby being more widely available); by the prevailing belief that the nation was best-served by making sure that each class of student received appropriate education to fit its members for the tasks they were expected to perform rather than one which aped social superiors, and by anxiety about maintaining social divisions through experiences in the education system.

Of course, the infrastructure of social division was not constructed solely on the basis of keeping upper-class children in school longer than lower- or middle-class children. There had to be visible differences in the three kinds of education meted out determining the route which the pupil took through school, and in all likelihood, ever after. Different syllabuses were drawn up; working-class children were merely taught to read, those of the upper and middle classes were led on to full literacy. Added to this was the erection of different goals of reading for each group. These goals can be related to the low status of children's literature generally, and the difference in status of books for children of different sex and class.

One effect of state-controlled education was to institutionalise language.[34] There thus became a division between the naturally acquired language of home, and the taught 'official' language of school. This led to problems in dealing with material at school: problems which were likely to be exaggerated for the child from a working-class home, 'where the vernacular varied so much from standard English that a reading lesson presented the difficulties normally encountered in the learning of a foreign language'.[35]

Part of the institutionalisation of language involved the setting up of educational milestones, for instance, a certified standard of reading.[36] The nature of these markers changed significantly between primary and secondary school. The child's initial encounters with 'correct' language took place in the primary school, where the emphasis was placed on grammar and the linguistic models were based on what is known as 'synthetic' or 'concrete' language.[37] This kind of speech and writing is stripped of literary qualities, concentrating instead on objects and experiences from everyday life. Accordingly, the child was encouraged to focus on the content of the text and not the form. Only those pupils advancing to secondary school came into contact with literary language as part of the curriculum.

The advent of formally organised and controlled language, with standard English as its ideal, highlighted the significance of the kind and amount of English taught as an indicator of class. Furthermore, the imposition of standard English created the possibility of conflict between the language used at home and in the street from that used within the institution. As the differences between the 'natural' language of the working classes was likely to be more pronounced than that of the upper classes (who both experienced education longer and had an established tradition of education, resulting in standard English being more or less the language of home and society), their experience of this conflict was inevitably stronger.

Moreover, the ability to use both standard English and literary language was, during this period, increasingly recognised to be akin to social power, for school defined not only what should be taught, how, when, and where it was taught, but also what knowledge was. The following extract from a 1910 Board of Education circular encapsulates attitudes which had increasingly been influencing the teaching of English in secondary schools and which had a direct bearing on the kind of linguistic education received by children of different classes.

> The instruction in English in a Secondary School aims at training the mind to appreciate English Literature, and at cultivating the power of using English Language in speech and writing. These objects are equally important, and each implies the other. Without training in the use of language, literature cannot be fully understood or properly appreciated. *Without the study of literature, there can be no mastery over language.*[38] [my italics]

Examination of these different educations helps to show further how the institutionalisation of language worked to maintain existing social divisions. Such educational policies were also instrumental in the creation of audiences, grouped by class and gender, within children's fiction, and thus contributed to the emergence of two categories within the genre. While it is necessary to be cautious about making too crude a generalisation, these categories can usefully be considered in the following way. One group became the 'canonised' literature, of which parents, teachers, and others in authority approved, both on the grounds of subject and literary merit. The other, 'uncanonised', literature was deemed objectionable in content and its denigrators denied it had any literary merit.[39] While in canonised works there operates a notion of dual readership – they simultaneously appeal to adult and child readers – in uncanonised fiction adult approval is not sought. One result of this schism is that canonised books tend to be dictated by educational constraints, while the uncanonised respond to commercial. It is thus usually the uncanonised books which comprise the best-selling, popular fiction, within the category of juvenile publishing.[40]

The relationship between perceived literary merit and intended audience is highly significant, for it would seem that works were accorded high or low status principally on the basis of their readership. This can in some measure be explained by returning to the influence of schooling on class and gender, and specifically to the child's institutional experience of literature.

The different experiences of language teaching for the three classes were essentially of duration and intention. Initial instruction for all three groups concentrated on establishing standard English as the language of education and authority. The average working-class pupil, leaving school at the age of 14, was destined not to progress beyond this level of instruction. S/he was introduced to the concept of language as the indicator of educational and social superiority and was likely to remain at the level of linguistic skill officially achieved at the time of leaving. As literature, the acknowledged source of mastery over language, was not introduced into the elementary-school curriculum, the 'muscular Briton' tended to find his/her 'appropriate' education had instilled linguistic skills which were pre-literary. These reflected reading and writing instruction based on concrete language, and which accordingly consciously excluded literary qualities. The kind of fiction directed at such readers is similarly devoid of literary attributes, trying instead to appear 'natural' and direct.[41] It is largely for this reason that realism has been and remains the narrative strategy of all popular children's fiction.[42]

Students who went on to the Board of Education secondary schools moved beyond this restricted experience of institutional language as their syllabus included the study of some English authors. The result of this inclusion was long-term and profound, for it led to a revival of classicism in upper-class education. This retreat into the classics was in part a by-product of the redefinition of full literacy which was required once universal, compulsory education came into force. It demonstrated that the education given to the lower and middle classes was not the same as that received by their social superiors. In addition, it reserved experience of classical literature, the yardstick of literary excellence, for a select few; thus, while those attending secondary schools might have been made familiar with a small amount of English literature, their knowledge and mastery of educated discourse was nevertheless shown to be incomplete.[43] The linguistic hierarchy was thus satisfactorily maintained.

The social pressures influencing the teaching of English divided readers into two categories: the elementary or concrete, and the cultured.[44] These divisions parallel notions of low- and high-status books for children. The cultured reader is associated with, 'a classic children's literary culture . . . largely dominated by the adult market (literary tradition)', while the concrete is identified with the emergence of, 'an autonomous children's literature which was being negatively identified with aspects of working-class culture'.[45] Relating this formulation to issues surrounding public and private reading practices and to the debates surrounding the spread of literacy, it is possible to begin to see the way in which a study of the evolution of juvenile publishing can help to cast new light on some of the dominant constructions of class, and crucially of gender.

The unease generated by the idea of a literate working class was countered by policies which made it more attractive for publishers to provide low-status, popular fiction on a grand scale. These apparently contradictory pressures resulted in a curious phenomenon. Working-class youth was introduced to the concept of officially approved, 'good', literature at school, but provided with cheap, plentiful, and exciting fiction elsewhere. This established the possibility of widely divergent 'public' (i.e. that done at school or under the aegis of other adult sources of authority) and 'private' (that read for pleasure) reading practices. This disparity is unusual in that it can be interpreted as servicing the needs of each social group; particularly with regard to the reading habits of the poor. The prevailing explanation for the disparity between the public and private reading habits of working-class children is based on the idea of cultural deprivation: if the poor were better educated, their taste would develop. In the nineteenth century this philosophy was opposed by those who viewed the spiral created by increased literacy as one which circled relentlessly downwards. Reading 'the unauthoritative, undignified, un-learned' publications, they believed, would only create a taste for more of the same.[46] In either case, the starting assumption was the same: the lower classes chose inferior reading matter because they knew no better.

An alternative explanation is that the lower classes were not *deprived* of culture, but had a *different* culture, and were consciously resisting middle-class language, values and tastes by choosing to read what were described as 'cheap' and 'sensational' publications.[47]

A more satisfactory interpretation, which takes account of both of the above as well as the social meaning of literacy, is that the private reading of the lower classes served two purposes. First, it provided escapist fantasies which kept the readers entertained, and was yet a passive activity (while they were reading, they could not be politically active). For this reason it was necessary to ensure that antipathies were not fed nor insurrection incited in the reading material to which they had most access. Such material was closely monitored, and fre-quently concern was expressed, for instance, that some fanta-sies might inspire 'copycat' acts of violence, vandalism, or intimidation.[48]

The second function served by popular literature was to reinforce the cultural superiority of those who condemned it. Just as the school was designed to maintain the status quo by providing different and suitable curricula and experiences for the different classes and sexes, so there was a need for a mass literature which would highlight the distance between it, and that read by the educated élite. The existence of popular fiction therefore made it possible for there to be widespread and detailed arguments about the level of cultural impoverishment they represented, which essentially served to elevate those to whom they were not directed and who purported to find them distasteful. The strength of this argument can best be seen by looking at the anxiety produced when the wrong class of child was discovered to be a regular reader of cheap fiction. There was a widespread conviction that, 'schoolboys or students who took to novel reading . . . never made much progress in after life'.[49] Salmon documents this concern with tales of

> very decent lads . . . who should have been at some ordinary boarding school, but instead of studying Euclid and Delectus, their readings had been of the 'Jack Sheppard' and 'Claude Duval' style of literature in the penny-dreadfuls, and they were now in Newgate awaiting their trial for burglary and half murdering an old house-keeper in some city offices.[50]

On a less violent score, Salmon, a self-appointed guardian of decent fiction for children, tells of

> some half-dozen lads . . . who, after reading a boys' weekly – a copy of which had carefully been included in their cargo – started off in an open boat down the Thames on their way to Australia! When caught they were found to have provided themselves with revolver, powder, shot, and biscuits. The crew of the Lilliputian barque *were sons of respectable parents*.[51] [my italics]

The fact that the ruling, educated élite ran a sustained campaign to devalue the fiction published for the entertainment of the working classes, while nevertheless allowing it to flourish, does not mean that this fiction was foisted off on or without value to its intended audience. If one of the principal effects of compulsory education was to institutionalise language, then a fundamental way of resisting the drive towards conformity would be to mount resistance at the level of language. Children might be required to attend school, and while there made to obey the rules and acknowledge that standard English was the correct form of language, but once outside school, they could demonstrate their independence by speaking and reading in the vernacular. In so doing, working-class pupils set themselves apart from their middle- and upper-class counterparts, but at the same time, they were propping up the existing hegemonic structure. Thus, popular fiction can be said to have served the needs of all social groups.

When read by only the working classes, then, the uncanonised fiction could be claimed by those in power to have positive social functions. The problem was that the popular fiction turned out to be exactly what its name implies, and young readers of *all* classes were found to be devotees of the cheap and sensational books and periodicals. When it became apparent that public school boys were regular readers of the 'literature of rascaldom',[52] the dichotomy between the public and private reading habits of the middle and upper classes attracted increased attention and caused censure to be directed at these low-status publications. Cultural decay and degeneracy were forecast, and a hyperbolised mythology of the fatal effects of novel reading on young men evolved. The result was the intervention of adults in the private reading of children (something which had been virtually unnecessary when choice was more limited). They began to define more specifically what constituted acceptable and unacceptable reading matter. This inevitably led to a more complex system of classification and consequently stimulated and elevated the industry of the literary critics of children's books, advising parents and teachers on the suitability of reading matter for children.

SEX

After the passage of the 1870 Education Act, a child's experience of school was increasingly likely to be shaped by gender as well as class.[53] Prior to that time, and particularly in schools organised by and for the working-class population, sexual separation existed notionally, but was casually administered. The Statistical Survey of 1830 observed: 'Though the schools are classed as Girls' and Boys' Schools, there are very few in which the sexes are entirely divided; almost every Boys' School containing some girls, and every Girls' School a few boys.'[54] Moreover, the working-class schools tended to minimise distinctions further, often providing precisely the same syllabus for girls as for boys (this, however, did not mean increased intellectual content; indeed, more often all the pupils learned to knit and sew as well as to read and cipher).[55]

As the government became more directly involved in schooling, there was increased insistence on formal structures, and among these, sexual division was prominent. Girls began to be disadvantaged (hitherto their chances of attending school regularly may have been slim, but once there, at least at primary level, their education would have been substantially the same as that of their male cohort).[56] After 1870 the Board School curriculum was increasingly organised along sexist lines, with girls being taught domestic subjects such as home economics, sewing, cookery and child care, while boys were offered new options such as animal physiology, algebra, chemistry, and physics. Physical separation, too, was more likely after 1870, and where separate schools were not provided, separate rooms and departments were.[57]

Once separate syllabuses for girls and boys became the norm, girls who managed to go on to a secondary school found that they were receiving instruction which was intellectually inferior to that provided for boys; it had a practical rather than an academic basis. (This distinction is, of course, relative, for boys' secondary education was, in precisely the same way, deemed to be inferior to that of public schools because it was supposed primarily to be vocational rather than scholarly.) This sexual discrimination within the educational system was to have repercussions on the form and status of fiction for girls and boys. It also helps to explain why the devaluation of girls' reading tends to be based more on gender than on class.

Girls had more leisure at the end of the century than boys and fewer ways of filling it. This was true even of working-class girls, for the worsening economic situation both resulted in fewer opportunities for work and led to social pressures which gave rise to a widespread retreat into the home.[58] In marked contrast to boys' reading, the reading of fiction was regarded as a suitable pastime for young women, as long as what they read was not considered to be challenging to the status quo or corrupting in any way. Moreover, unlike boys, girls were often

24

encouraged to read and study literature at school. This policy became more pronounced in the early decades of the twentieth century, with the division between the sexes being exaggerated by the fact that styles of teaching for boys and girls were also different. English lessons for boys attempted to treat the subject scientifically, and thus, even in the state schools, retained some allegiance to the methods and concerns derived from the teaching of the classics. Boys learned English language skills: grammar, syntax, etc., while girls were encouraged to concentrate on the creative aspects of the subject: literature and composition.[59]

Thus, most girls were encouraged to read and even to write, but the activity was separated from academic disciplines and, just as their abilities and areas of study tended to be dismissed as inferior to those of boys, so what they read was regarded as frivolous and classed as low-status, popular fiction. So it is that the largest area within juvenile publishing, books written specifically for girls, and the largest and most avid group of readers, girls (a term which in late-Victorian and Edwardian England could encompass an age range the upper limit of which was twenty-five), were consistently ridiculed by teachers, critics, and journalists, and their authors discredited, at least in terms of literary standing. Compare this attitude to that which pertained to fiction for boys.

Just as boys at school were regarded as requiring more rigorous courses of study and were generally accorded privileged intellectual status, so the books written specifically for boys were not instantly dismissed, classed as 'juvenile', and in the process devalued as literature in the same way that books for their sisters almost invariably were. Moreover, the value attached to fiction for boys tended to be more determined by class considerations than was fiction for girls. In this way 'bloods', penny-dreadfuls, and sensational novels seem to have been panned because they were regarded as publications suitable for working-class youth, not because they were intended for consumption by boys.

At the opposite pole of fiction produced for boys is the adventure tale. The success of adventure stories provides evidence that stratification was based as much on sex as class, for the boys' adventure story appealed so strongly to adults that books in this genre were frequently and enthusiastically read by men. In his study of the boys' school tale (which for a time had equal standing with the adventure tale, but rapidly degenerated), Musgrave suggests that such tales were written for a dual readership (boys and men) and achieved their objective so successfully that at times the two readerships merged and adults read books ostensibly written for boys, and boys similarly were readers of books written for men.[60]

The criteria which determined what made a good adventure story were very different from those which pertained in most other areas of juvenile fiction (the boys' school story being in some cases an exception). While most fiction for young people earned the appellation 'good' if it had a strong moral and educational content, the adventure story was considered to be good if it trespassed into the adult domain of literary quality. This meant that unlike most children's fiction, the boys' adventure story was endowed with the powers of innovation and permitted to deal with subjects which would not necessarily have been deemed suitable. These exceptions were part and parcel of the sophisticated use of the notion of dual readership, and boys were not, therefore, expected to be cognisant of the gamut of references and literary devices identified by their fathers (I use 'boys' here as an indicator of intended audience rather than actual readership, for girls were known to be devoted readers of the adventure story from its inception).

To the best of my knowledge, the phenomenon of adults annexing books written for girls is unknown. Occasionally books written by authors who were regarded primarily as writers for girls were reclassified into areas of higher status, namely biblical or historical tales, or books about bourgeois family life, which often include fantastical elements. These books (among them works such as C. M. Yonge's *The Daisy Chain*, 1856; Louisa May Alcott's *Little Women*, 1868; and Carroll's 'Alice' stories, 1865 and 1872) were read by children of both sexes and comprise the bulk of the canonised area of juvenile fiction during the period under discussion. Indeed, many of them are regarded as the 'children's classics' of our own day. None of these books, however, would be described as exclusively 'girls' stories', even though they may originally have been intended for a female audience and may appear to have the same concerns as other books written for girls and young women.

Thus stratification of books within the field of juvenile publishing follows, or perhaps responds to, divisions within the education system. The following chapters look at the implications of this hierarchy for juvenile fiction and its readers, and endeavour to discover how what is read contributes to the formation of class and gender identifications.

Chapter 2

Sexuality and status in juvenile fiction

> *In the discussion of children's fiction, I repeatedly come across the most emphatic of refusals or demands: that there should be no disturbance at the level of language, no challenge to our sexuality, no threat to our status as critics, and no question of our relation to the child.*

> (Jacqueline Rose, *The Case of Peter Pan or the Impossibility of Children's Fiction*, p. 20)

Children's literature and the image of childhood

Thus far I have concentrated on the social and economic pressures which affected the growth and development of juvenile publishing in the late nineteenth and early twentieth centuries. It is now time to consider the recipient of these publishing products – the child reader – in order to understand the significance of early changes in the style and content of books for young readers for the perception of cultural roles. What becomes apparent is that a tension pervades juvenile publishing as a consequence of an unresolved conflict between the child's psychic needs, the adult's insistence on the genre's allegiance to traditions of instruction and socialisation, the adult's tendency to use children's literature to recover the past and as a safe arena for fantasy, and, finally, the commercial dictates of the publishing industry.

Up to now, I have been concerned with all aspects of juvenile publishing and with all kinds of young readers. I shall return to a consideration of low-status literature in later chapters, but at this point my concern is primarily with what must be regarded as essentially middle-class publications. The reason for this is that while there are stratifications within children's literature (some of which were considered in the previous chapter), as a genre it has always been almost entirely middle class in subject matter and values. The middle-class nature of juvenile fiction is paradoxical: while the majority of books published for children appear to be aimed at an audience which is rural, affluent, and sexually immature, most young people are from urban, working-class homes and are preoccupied with attaining sexual maturity.[1]

These demographics would also have been largely true of late-Victorian and Edwardian youth. In fact, contemporary middle- and upper-class concern over the social problems caused by the large numbers of young people (mostly working-class) suddenly finding themselves living in an urban environment may have been a major factor in the evolution of the solidly middle-class nature of books directed at young people.[2] Certainly the middle-class nature of juvenile publishing seems to reflect the fact that the genre came to fruition in the second half of the nineteenth century, when the economic and social stability and power of the bourgeois population were being consolidated. As a body of literature it has traditionally served the needs of that one class.[3] This is in itself a source of tension, for while children's literature *is* dominated by middle-class values, concerns and images, it is read by children of every class. Moreover, the middle-class nature of the content tends to dominate both the most and least respected children's books, which means that even when a book has been deliberately directed at working-class children, it nevertheless maintains its middle-class basis.[4]

A final, related, factor which contributed to the middle-class nature of juvenile publishing came from the dominant, bourgeois, notion of childhood being elaborated at the end of the nineteenth century. The need for a special literature for children could only be perceived when children were recognised as being different from adults. As Ariès says in *Centuries of Childhood*, this process had begun by the end of the seventeenth century. By the late nineteenth century, not only did a fully-formed middle- and upper-class notion of childhood exist, but surrounding it there had also evolved an idealised, highly sentimental aureole. Possibly in reaction to the new pressures and rapid changes which were occurring in the work place and society, the bourgeois home and family came to be regarded as citadels: the last bastions of civilisation holding out against the menace and corruption of the marketplace and a fallen world. As part of this process, childhood provided a peculiarly potent symbol of purity and innocence.[5]

The child in late-Victorian art and literature reflected a notion of childhood concerned with helping to identify and resolve the problems of middle-class adults. The image of childhood was simultaneously sentimental, escapist, the repository of all that was good and pure, and also the domain of covert desires and fantasies. This last area pertains as much to the writing of work ostensibly for children as to images of children and childhood contained in the arts and letters of the period.[6]

There have been a number of attempts to explain the sudden surge of highly imaginative writing classified as 'juvenile' which was generated in Britain at this time. It has been suggested that this collective adult use of childhood indicates that children's literature was regarded by some well-established authors as a safe venue for adult fantasies because, being innocent, children were incorruptible, and therefore the fantasies (in which the erotic quest is metamorphosed into a quest for adventure) could not hurt them.[7]

This explanation disregards the fact that the fantasies described as providing a release for adults were also highly popular with children. Attention has been focused on the adult writer and on the corpus of juvenile writing within literature; not on the child reader. This has been the critical tradition outside the worlds of education and psychoanalysis. While it is important thus to elaborate a major component in the process of appealing to dual readerships, it is always necessary to remember that the appeal of fantasy and of the entire text are different for the experienced adult reader and the apprentice child reader.[8] Adult interest and approval are important in making a book's literary reputation, but they are unreliable indicators of the success a book will enjoy with children. It is, of course, impossible to say specifically what any reader or class of reader demands or experiences from books (reading is a private and subjective process about which it is difficult to obtain reliably reproducible evidence); however, certain assumptions based on current understanding of linguistics and the psyche make it possible to discuss the reading experience in terms of intellectual, cognitive, and psychological development, and to relate this to existing theories of childhood. This enhances the understanding of how the insertion of books for juveniles, and especially juvenile fiction, into the established publishing world during this time has affected the subsequent development of that area of the publishing industry and the impact of its products on children.

The young reader

Although the nineteenth century saw the celebration of the family, domestic life and a concomitant focus on children and childhood, it also saw a schism created between the child and its family by legislation which ensured that at least some part of childhood would be spent in school. There was a dramatic increase in the number of middle-class families that dispatched their male offspring to boarding schools. With their insistence on tradition and their determination to make themselves exclusive by means of codes which distinguished 'insiders' from 'outsiders', these institutions greatly increased the degree and quality of the separation of child from family. Ariès suggests that boarding schools were crucial to the development of a separate literature for children because they created distance between the worlds of adult and child and questioned the suitability of shared themes and literatures.[9] This process of questioning was instrumental in subtly changing the concept of childhood from one in which adult needs were paramount, to one which was intensely concerned with the needs of the child.[10]

As the concept of childhood changed, so theories about the child's reading experience were revised and elaborated, and a rationale for the production of special books for children developed. By 1890 Edward J. Salmon could justify the existence of the genre, in spite of continued debates over its merits, by evoking the current concept of childhood. The young reader was acknowledged to have skills and requirements which were different from (and in some ways perhaps

33

superior to) those of his/her parents or teachers: 'The chief reason which prompts me to support a special literature for boys and girls is that such a literature is necessary. The young mind should be nourished on food specially prepared for it just as much as the young body.'[11] Salmon continues his speculations by decrying those who would fill the child with inappropriate adult information and cares: 'Thank Heaven nature is all powerful, and in the vast majority of cases children are children and will remain children.[12]

Here is the notion that not only do children enjoy the books written for them, but that these books also serve a purpose. Salmon goes on to describe juvenile fiction as a useful halfway house in which the young reader consolidates skills and acquires experience until fit to progress to more mature works. However, the tendency during this period was still to regard good children's books as aids to correct socialisation. They therefore had to be clearly instructive, elevating, and sexually appropriate. Although a discourse about the psychic needs of the child (usually revolving around the value of the imagination) was beginning to be heard, at this crucial time in the development of juvenile publishing there was insufficient vocabulary and theoretical structure with which to question the nature of the categories and divisions which were becoming the hard edges of the genre. It is perhaps only with a combination of hindsight and recent work in developmental psychology, psychoanalysis, structural linguistics and sociology that the significance of publishing decisions (whether deliberate, accidental, or the result of inertia) can be fully appreciated.

The principal point I wish to make here is that before the full importance of childhood influences was realised, when childhood was seen as an incubation period during which miniature adults were stuffed with food, information, and attitudes with which to become fully-developed adults, or was used as an escape for disaffected adults, the ambition of publishers and those adults involved in introducing books to children was primarily to provide literature which would help to school the reader in the manners and mores of society. While such books might have within them the structures and material which made for satisfying reading experiences, these were rarely identified or perceived as desirable qualities in themselves.

It seems likely that the emerging image of childhood was greatly affected by the needs of the publishing industry and by the well-intentioned contributions made by those who wrote in the capacity of authorities on children's books. As the industry boomed and titles proliferated, there was great concern over how to deal with all its products. Publishers' catalogues became increasingly categorised and their attempts to direct potential purchasers to the section of the market where they were most likely to find works suitable for boys and girls of various ages and classes can be seen in handbooks like Charlotte M. Yonge's *What Books to Lend and What to Give* and Edward J. Salmon's *Juvenile Literature as it is* (both published in 1888). In such publications, the authors attempted to separate the good from the bad and to recommend books on the basis of age, sex, and class. Both authors recommend only solidly middle-class books and periodicals, roundly condemning every variety and relation of the 'Jack Sheppard literature' (i.e. bloodthirsty thrillers), the appeal of which they do not seek to understand.

Yonge's division of books is revealing. Below the age of ten she makes no distinction between books for boys and girls. Roughly at the onset of puberty these categories come into play. At this time, she notes, girls will continue to read any kind of book, but boys will not read books which seem to be directed at girls. By 1880 then, girls' books are coming to be seen as those which boys will not read, an important step towards classifying them as works of lower status and so of attributing to girls the need for an inferior literature. Moreover, the activities of debate, publication and categorisation were contributing to the creation of firm notions about what made suitable books for the different groups, which in turn gave rise to reliance on formulaic structures and content.

The fact that, 'girls and young women are for the most part indiscriminate devourers of fiction'[13] led to problems which shall be discussed in Chapters 5 and 6. The effect on boys' reading and the subsequent social consequences may have been equally profound; especially as these correspond to initial problems and pressures surrounding successful and stable gender identification. That these divisions, and particularly the censorship of anything deemed 'unmanly', were not innate to juvenile literature can perhaps most clearly be seen by looking at the changes which took place in writing for boys in the quarter of a century separating such early works as Hughes's *Tom Brown's Schooldays* (1857) and Farrar's *Eric, or, Little By Little* (1858), and the comparable boys' school stories Talbot Baines Reed was writing in the 1880s. The central characters in the earlier books weep, twine arms, exchange gifts of flowers and bestow kisses in a way which would have appalled any fictional headmaster after Reed had provided the impetus and pattern for writing about life at school in *The Fifth Form at St. Dominics* (1881). In the preface to this work, written by G. A. Hutchinson (editor of the *Boys' Own Paper* in which the story first appeared in serial form), this contrast was identified and celebrated. Hutchinson declared that Reed's boys

> stand at the antipodes alike of an effeminate sentimentality – the paragons who prate platitudes and die young – and of the morbid specimens of youthful infamy only too frequently paraded by the unreal sensationalism of today to meet the cravings of a vitiated taste.[14]

Even the trio of Beetle, M'Turk, and Stalky in Kipling's *Stalky & Co.* (1899), whose time at school is largely spent waging a sustained campaign against many of the established traditions of the public school (and occasionally waving the slightly suspect banner of literature and art to attract the charges of their muscle-bound, philistine cohort and predominantly mulish instructors), hold to ideals of manliness and patriotism. They regularly revile the pusillanimous Eric after receiving a copy of Farrar's book as a gift. Their rejection of *Eric* is indicative of the narrowing of what was considered suitable for boys. When Charlotte M. Yonge declared that, 'boys especially should not have childish tales with weak morality or "washy" piety; but should have heroism and nobleness kept before their eyes,' and that, 'true manhood needs, above all earthly qualities, to be impressed upon them',[15] she was both uttering and influencing contemporary attitudes which became entrenched in publishing practice.

The gendering of the reader

Yonge's concern that boys read the right kind of book is indicative of a belief that young men needed to be firmly encouraged to conform to the prevailing definition of masculinity. The resulting pressure had many sources and took many forms, but at this point it is important to underline the changes which surrounded boys' reading, for they were peculiarly effective and enduring.

Their potency is not exclusively derived from the representation of masculinity characteristic of books for boys, but from the combination of this representation with the general range of boys' reading. Boys were not just given positive role models in their books, but were directed away from the kind of reading matter which explored the uncertain worlds of emotions and relationships. What they were given instead were books which posited a predictable, knowable world by supplying information and answers and suppressing problematic personal questions. The significance of this needs to be understood in terms of both external social pressures and of the psyche, for while it is possible to explain the reasons for changes in what is read as directly resulting from the material world, their consequences are largely internal. This is due in part to the private nature of the act of reading and the possibilities for fantasy much literature provides. Perhaps more important is the fact that books are rooted in language and, especially for the child, such encounters with language are central to the development of an image of the self.

Today books have to compete with a variety of media which provide related opportunities for fantasy and language development, but for the child growing up in late-Victorian and Edwardian England, they provided the most widely available opportunity for experimenting with language. For this reason, the narrowing of the notion of what constituted acceptable reading matter for boys is important, for the child reader is not just filling in time between youth and maturity. Reading is one way in which the child learns about social organisation; what is read can affect how s/he understands herself or himself socially. In addition, the fact that boys generally read less than girls (which may be a consequence of what it is they feel they are permitted to read) may adversely affect how they understand themselves, for reading is part of the process of acquiring language.[16] Young readers are serving an apprenticeship – are acquiring linguistic knowledge through trying out different constellations of words which writers have used to articulate experience. In the process, they become acquainted with a variety of specialised discourses which help them to evaluate and differentiate their thoughts – and especially their thoughts about themselves. According to Moffat (1968), children

> utter themselves almost entirely through stories – real or invented – and they apprehend what others say through story. The young learner . . . talks and reads about characters, events and settings [which are] charged with symbolic meaning because they are tokens standing for unconscious classes and postulations of experience.[17]

Thus stories can be likened to dreams, for the things they contain are not always what they seem and each reader uses emblems selfishly in order to resolve individual problems and overcome personal anxieties. The young reader's inexperience dramatically affects the reading process. Because s/he has not yet read many books, the reading experience is very potent. The young reader has not yet learnt to recognise conventions and to distance herself or himself from the printed word. This lack of distance means that the child reader reads herself or himself into the text.[18] Consequently, the different characters in a story may be functioning as different aspects of the self (male/female, good/bad, etc.) and through the processes of splitting and displacement emotions can be clarified and personality integration facilitated.

38

There are other characteristics of children's reading which shape texts. For instance, the satisfying ending, which is regarded with suspicion in serious fiction for adults, is a necessary feature in publishing for juveniles. The Swiss educational philosopher, Jean Piaget, has proposed a model of the child as innately moral. Accordingly, the child reader requires that books have endings in which the good are rewarded and the bad, if not punished, at least diminished. (They are not always overcome but may be marginalised, humiliated, lose a weapon or source of power.)[19] It is only with increased and successful experience of the world and of texts that this need is reduced. Similarly, the child reader may have problems dealing with abstractions. S/he tends to accept those features of a text which seem tangibly, concretely, right and therefore meaningful.[20]

In addition to these characteristics of children's reading is the fact that during the reading process the child is trying out and acquiring discourses which enable thought about the self. Lacan used ideas from structural linguistics in his reading of Freud to elaborate a theory in which personality is shown to be a product of language. The acquisition of language, he suggests, involves a shift from the essentially instinctual, inchoate and incommunicable mode of relating to the world which he calls the Imaginary order, to the formed and articulate Symbolic order. This shift enables communication and the possibility of social relationships. It is at the point when the shift from the predominantly Imaginary to the predominantly Symbolic way of relating to the world occurs that Lacan identifies the self as becoming divided. The Imaginary order continues to exist and to generate desires which elude language and so cannot become conscious. Lacan thus focuses attention on the idea that it is only possible to think about yourself through language. One aspect of such thought is learning the different subject positions which contribute to identity (he, she, boy, girl, etc.). Equally, the world is only able to be understood through discourse. Reading, and especially the reading of literature, helps to teach subject positions and to acquaint the reader with a multiplicity of discourses. As Catherine Belsey observes:

If we accept Lacan's analysis of the importance of language in the construction of the subject, it becomes apparent that literature as one of the most persuasive uses of language may have an important influence on the ways in which people grasp themselves and their relation to the real relations in which they live.[21]

Clearly, then, for the child, reading can make fundamental contributions to the way in which s/he understands the world and herself/himself within it. According to Freud, the most important feature which goes into this understanding is the identification with a particular sexual role. Of course, by the time the child is able to read independently s/he will already have made crucial sexual identifications. The reading experience is, therefore, essentially one of identification, confirmation, and repetition. Nevertheless, gender positions are not rigidly fixed and they continue to be influenced by the kind of language available to and used by the subject. Accordingly, when publishers and critics began to separate books for boys from books for girls, they profoundly affected the reading experience, and consequently an important part of the identification with a sexual role for children of both sexes.

There is evidence that the end of the nineteenth century, when juvenile fiction was coming into vogue, was a time when people were becoming more concerned with gender, probably as part of a larger obsession with the notion of sexuality as an indicator of social acceptability and status. The desire to define and control any aspect of society usually indicates the presence of challenge and/or disturbance. When considering nineteenth-century attitudes toward sexual difference it is usual to focus on the pressures and problems surrounding girls and women, but boys too were the subjects of analysis and control. At this time (for reasons which will be discussed in detail shortly), masculinity became both more valued and more elusive than ever before and this inevitably resulted in a devaluation of femininity. The sociologist Nancy Chodorow has investigated the structures and conditions of sexual difference today. Many of her observations about the nature and perpetuation of gender roles seem to have their origins in this late-Victorian obsession with gender and I have found them useful for identifying how and why the rigid and exaggerated sexual ideals of juvenile fiction came into being and the social and psychic consequences of their continuation.

There are a number of areas in which Chodorow's thesis is open to debate; nevertheless, many of the points she raises in *The Reproduction of Mothering* are convincingly argued and are useful when considering the relationship between reading habits and the formation of sexual identity. Of particular significance to this discussion is the emphasis she places on the learned nature of masculinity. This sheds light on why boys' reading matter is so prescriptive, why boys read what they do, why they read so much less than girls and why they read so little fiction.

According to Chodorow, masculinity is less available and accessible to boys than femininity as represented by their mothers.[22] Chodorow's understanding of masculinity is very much coloured by her thesis that in order to break the cycle by which the existing patriarchal society reproduces itself, it is necessary to change the infant's relationship with its primary caretaker. Her analysis focuses on the mother/infant relationship and develops a profile which shows how, through her handling of and responses to children of different sex, the mother-figure tends to perpetuate the asymmetrical power-relationships between males and females characteristic of patriarchy. The result of typical mothering, she says, is to produce girls whose destiny is likely to be domestic, and who will generally find themselves allocated to (and accepting) social positions which are inferior to males, and boys who, while socially confident and successful, are incapable of forming affective relationships and of nurturing.

Chodorow's thesis minimises the influences of biology and deliberate role training. Rather, she sees the reproduction of existing modes of mothering as the consequence of 'social, structurally induced, psychological processes', by which she means that the potential for mothering and the affective relationships it entails exist in all infants but are only developed through a combination of such things as handling, address, environment, expectation, and cultural organization.[23] These are different for children of different sex because the structures (now obsolete) of society dictate that they will be. The result is that girls develop relationally, while boys' capacities for relationships are stunted in favour of such qualities as separateness – the ability to be separate, to separate from others, to work independently and be less concerned about others – and individuality, which work to enhance their chances of succeeding socially, in terms of money, power, prestige. It also means that women are inevitably colluding in the continuation of male dominance.

In order to explain the ways in which children usually acquire the desire to conform to sexual roles typically associated with their biological sex, Chodorow considers the nature and implications of what Freud termed the Oedipal phase. Chodorow departs from Freud in her emphasis on object relations and ego development in the formation of sexual identity rather than on sexuality as dominated by the libido.[24] This leads to the main area of difference between them: Chodorow's contention that it is more difficult to achieve masculinity than femininity. Freud perceived the girl child as having the more difficult task. To support her conclusion, Chodorow provides evidence about initial environmental experience to which she adds observations about current social organisation, which tends to result in fathers being absent from home more than they are present. This means that in acquiring his sexual identity, the male child is now guided more through his recognition of the fact that he is different from the mother than through identification with his father. This emphasis on difference means that the movement towards masculinity requires the male child to see himself apart, and as an individual. Chodorow concludes that, 'in male-dominated, father-absent societies, masculinity and sexual difference are intertwined with issues of separation and individuation almost from the beginning of a boy's life.'[25]

These elements: the taught nature of masculinity and the way in which masculine identity is grounded in difference, often at the expense of affective relationships, can be used to help explain the restriction embargoes and taboos surrounding boys' reading. It also sheds light on the tendency for girls' books to be regarded as inferior. The effort required to achieve a masculine sexual identity causes masculinity itself to be rigidly defined, and in pursuit of it a boy 'represses those qualities he takes to be feminine within himself, and rejects and devalues women and whatever he considers to be feminine in the social world.'[26] He needs to be able to recognise certain things as male and superior.

If true, it seems likely that Chodorow's thesis – that masculinity is unattainable and therefore boys idealise it while femininity is all too available and girls may need to escape from it, at least temporarily – would be reflected in the reading needs of boys and girls, and this seems to be the case. In *The Uses of Enchantment* Bruno Bettelheim has provided a model for viewing children's reading as functional. For him, the 'use of enchantment' is precisely to resolve the Oedipal phase. Girls' failure to do this may, therefore, account in part for their greater propensity to read, to read fiction almost exclusively and sometimes to read obsessively (aspects of female reading habits which will be developed in Chapter 5), for books constantly enact the Oedipal drama or provide outlets for fantasies surrounding unresolved Oedipal attachments. The corollary to this is that boys' reading tastes and habits appear to reflect the social drive to help them resolve the Oedipal phase and the need to sustain its resolution (which is always impermanent and unstable). Thus, where girls prefer to read fiction and fantasy, boys gravitate towards non-fictional works.[27] Additionally, when boys do read fiction, they tend to prefer works which are characterised by action and which are oriented towards exploration, mastery and confidence rather than those (the preferred choice of girls) concerned with examining relationships and internal states.[28] Thus, since the end of the last century the typical reading habits of boys and girls have tended to underline their social experience of what it is to be male or female. Through address, expectation, and content which provides an analogue for cultural organisation, boys are encouraged to become masculine and girls feminine.

The peculiarly language-based nature of the reading process means that books have the potential to do more than merely reproduce what the child experiences socially. Chodorow's work is not concerned with the ways in which language is involved in psychic organisation, but I perceive this to be a crucial factor in the formation of a sexual identity. Certainly in order to discuss the influence of what is read on the child's perception of his/her gender it is necessary to consider the relationship between language and sexuality in addition to the child's social environment.

Language, reading and sexual difference

Possibly as a consequence of the nature of their reading experience, boys generally read less and read less widely than girls; and it may be that as a result of this their verbal skills tend to develop later and they tend to require different things from language. These things have been true at least since the middle of the last century.[29] Paradoxically, the girl's very facility with language and her willingness to lose herself in fiction can be understood as symptomatic of her preparedness for assuming the conventional female role and an influential factor in the perpetuation of male dominance.[30]

The paradox is twofold. The most obvious contradiction lies in the association of verbal power with male education and authority (especially that gained through professions, institutions, and offices). Knowledge, training and position have traditionally rendered men more articulate in public situations or those in which information and presentation (ranging from acquired rhetorical flourishes to maximising the rational rather than emotional basis for an argument) are paramount. Women, through lack of education, opportunity and approbation, have historically been less likely to adapt their linguistic aptitudes for public contexts and so in some sense have been deprived of their ability to function at precisely the point at which their skills might make them superior.

The second feature of the paradox is more complex and lies in the centrality of language in the formation of sexual identity.

Lacan saw sexual difference as becoming important at the point of entry into the Symbolic order and identified the process with the insertion of the father into the mother-infant dyad. With the acquisition of language and the recognition of separateness it entails, Lacan says, the psychical structure is completely readjusted, for with language comes the *possibility* of liberation from the all-powerful but imaginary relationship with the mother.[31] The importance of the father in this process is reflected in the terminology Lacan coins: *nom du père* (name or law of the father). At this point the father (possessor of the phallus) is also identified as the representative of power; especially in the social world. The phallus for Lacan becomes the axis on which language and sexual identity depend; therefore, when the child is in the Oedipal phase and learning to accept his/her gender identity, the possession or lack of a phallus is crucial. Thus, where the boy's experience of difference from the mother leads to separateness and individuality, which enable him to assume a dominant role in the community, a girl's experience of difference from the father has the reverse effect. She is perceived and perceives herself as lacking the necessary means for obtaining power and can only obtain it symbolically.

Part of the same process is the creation of the unconscious, which for Lacan is both a product of language and structured like language: before language there is no subject and no unconscious, but only needs and instincts. It would seem, therefore, that the female tendency to take pleasure in language – to appreciate its multiple meanings and through literature to pursue what cannot be said or achieved in life – may in some way narrow the gap between the conscious and the unconscious, simultaneously reducing insistence on rationality and promoting fantasy. The consequences of such a state would be to encourage passivity and narcissism on the one hand, and on the other to create a greater perception of the gap between verbal skill and articulation than is experienced by the more limited exploration of language characterised as masculine.

Thus it can be said that girls' early linguistic abilities and literary experiences may make them verbally skilful while heightening their sense of what they cannot say. Their enjoyment of texts and ability to lose themselves in literature, instead of promoting a sense of mastery, recreates or maintains a state corresponding to the infant's initial dependence on the mother: passive, dependent, and possessing a limited sense of its ability to communicate. This is the second feature of the paradox of female linguistic facility.

Lacan's ideas about the value of texts are also helpful when discussing boys' and girls' reading habits. According to Lacan the value of reading lies in the text's ability to contain what is desired and to reveal it through metaphorical substitution and rhetorical displacement.[32] Just as an analyst interprets a patient's discourse to reveal what s/he actually desires, so the reader discovers beneath the surface meaning of a text another – the repressed – meaning. Experience can make the reader more skilful at identifying what is being revealed and how, but whether experienced or not, the reader is always bringing the unconscious to bear upon the text: the unconscious inevitably contributes to the manufacture of meaning.

It would seem, therefore, that Lacan's reader is in effect exercising the unconscious and that texts provide the possibility of verbal points of intersection for consciousness and the unconscious. Girls, generally more avid readers, are likely to experience more of these intersections than boys. Having said that, none of these habits, attitudes, experiences, or tendencies is unique to either sex. It is necessary always to remember that the qualities required for reading and responding in a particular way exist in readers of both sexes but are likely to be more pronounced in one or other, making it convenient to label them as 'masculine' or 'feminine' qualities. Not surprisingly, 'masculine' language, with its emphasis on rationality, empiricism and control, is valued in patriarchal societies. The internal, intuitive and fragmentary nature of 'feminine' language has traditionally been rejected as symptomatic of an inability to function in the real world of material relations.

The idea that there are two kinds of language and that one (the masculine) is more functional and more highly esteemed in male-dominated cultures, is of particular importance in understanding why the books written for children of different sex play such a significant role in the perpetuation of the existing social order. The kind of language used complements and reinforces the social structures and values represented in the stories. The sexually differentiated popular juvenile fiction which originated in the closing decades of the last century instructs the reader in the behaviour deemed acceptable and appropriate on the basis of sex, and addresses him/her in a way which is likely to confirm previous sexual identifications.

It is important to remember, however, that this process is not one way. While those responsible for producing and presenting books for young people may agree on the basic ingredients of a book suitable for children on the basis of their observations, experiences and beliefs, once given shape in literature these ingredients become able to exert an influence of their own. Moreover, the child reader will have unconsciously worked out a personal theory of gender and will use this, together with her/ his current concept of self, in the reading process. S/he is thus predisposed to respond to texts in certain ways. Finally, although I have been emphasising the ways in which a specific kind of juvenile fiction instructs readers in the prevailing attitudes toward sexual difference, it is necessary to underline the fact that books do not necessarily contain representations of masculinity/femininity which actually correspond to those likely to be encountered in the world. For instance, the popular fiction written between 1880–1910 contained characters who embodied the sexual *ideal*. Because of the persuasive powers of books outlined above, they can accustom readers to the ideas they contain about the world and about what the sexual ideal is. They may maintain or strengthen a prevailing belief, or reject it in favour of a new, or even an out-of-date, attitude. The tendency in books for boys during the period under discussion was to accelerate the movement in society toward a more 'manly' version of masculinity. When they became adults, the boys who had read these books themselves produced books which corresponded to their ideas (and personal approxima-tions) and passed them on to the next generation. This process continued more or less unimpeded for the better part of a century, and with each generation the historical precedent for equating masculinity with the late-Victorian/Edwardian ideal was more clearly established. (The same process of transmission applies equally to girls' fiction though, as will become evident in Chapters 5 and 6, the formative discourse was essentially reactionary and residual.)

As new media came into being, they frequently adopted the values, images and languages formerly associated with books. A typical example is found in the feature-length cartoons of Walt Disney, which were based on fairy tales, but were revised and expanded to provide unequivocal models of the ideal American hero and heroine. Because of this, identifying how attitudes to gender which came to prominence more than a hundred years ago have been perpetuated and elaborated in juvenile fiction can contribute to understanding a variety of material which introduces the child to ideas about social organisation. The following chapters look at the ways in which the content, structure and address of popular, nineteenth-century juvenile fiction written for the different sexes encourages boys to be masculine and girls to be feminine. Considering how these texts were regarded, together with their likely psychic implications for young readers, can help to explain the effect of reading modern books which are also written either for boys or girls. In particular, looking at the origins of the popular literature for the children of different sexes contributes to our understanding of why apparently obsolete gender roles have proved so difficult to revise.

Chapter 3

'Boys must be boys': masculinity and boys' reading habits

You may chisel a boy into shape, as you would a rock, or hammer him into it, if he is of a better kind, as you would a piece of bronze.

(John Ruskin, *Sesame and Lilies*, 1871)

'It's not brutality,' murmured little Hartopp, *as though answering a question no one had asked.* 'It's boy; only boy.'

(Rudyard Kipling, *Stalky & Co.*, 1899)

Fiction for boys at the end of the last century is markedly different from that at mid-century. The difference is essentially the result of a change in attitudes to and representations of masculinity. There is a hardening of what is meant by 'manliness', which reflects the ideological division of the sexes into entirely separate spheres of interest, operation, and behaviour. This division had prevailed for most of the century, but for reasons which will become apparent, was less insisted upon in fiction for boys at mid-century than it was in the final decades and at the beginning of the present century.

Ruskin encapsulated the differences between the masculine and feminine domains and the behaviour appropriate to each in his lecture, 'Of Queen's Gardens' (published as part of *Sesame and Lilies* in 1871). 'The man's power', he told his audience, 'is active, progressive, defensive. He is eminently the doer, the creator, the discoverer, the defender. His intellect is for speculation and invention; his energies for adventures, for war, and for conquest'.[1] In his dealings with the world, the lecturer went on to say, the man would at times be wounded, subdued, misled and, invariably, hardened. Ruskin's model man guarded his home (both domestic and national), secured its maintenance and assured its progress. By contrast, his ideal woman ruled over the home, securing its order, comfort and loveliness. She is passive and intuitive, ruling by example and praise.[2]

These are the models of masculinity and feminity codified in children's fiction at the time when juvenile publishing was becoming a recognised, separate branch of the industry. Fictional boys endeavoured to do: to explore, challenge and master. Girls in books aspired to ethereal benignity. Boy-heroes are characterised by rationality. They embody the masculine discourse by adhering strictly to empirical principles, and also in their ethos, which combines self-help with a high achievement orientation (indicated by economic success); once information has been obtained and facts assembled, then all that remains to ensure success is courage and athleticism. The language in late-Victorian and Edwardian books for boys is, therefore, direct and factual; it conveys information (ranging from the geological and geographical to the historical and botanical) and advances the plot rather than exploring emotions and relationships. Indeed, these belong to the domain of the female, and were therefore almost invariably excluded from boys' fiction (as were women).

These features had been present in the boys' adventure story from its inception, as evidenced by works such as Marryat's *Mr Midshipman Easy* (1836) and *Masterman Ready* (1841–2), Kingsley's *Westward Ho!* (1855) and Ballantyne's *Coral Island* (1858), but had not been insisted upon so vigorously. In fact, the heroes of such works often combined qualities later associated with femininity with masculine attributes such as rationality, strength, enterprise and courage. For instance, in his dedication to *Westward Ho!*, Kingsley describes the ideal of English virtue he is trying to portray as, 'at once manful and godly, practical and enthusiastic, prudent and self-sacrificing'. The less-than ideal Eustace Leigh (cousin to the hero, Amyas Leigh) in Kingsley's story is criticised in part for being incapable of love characterised by chivalry, self-sacrifice and purity. Self-sacrifice and purity became central components of the feminine ideal and were accordingly virtually excluded from most male characters in late-Victorian juvenile fiction.

In addition to the fact that the representation of masculinity in early adventure fiction for boys was less rigid than it became, it is significant that for most of the century such works were neither perceived nor marketed as the staple constituent of boys' fictional diets. Alongside the muscular and manly heroes who filled the pages of adventure books, boys were introduced to less materially successful youths. In religious tracts they read about young men who misspent their youths and those who were too good for this earth. Works such as *Tom Brown's Schooldays* and *Eric, or, Little by Little* explored relationships and permitted emotional displays. These alternatives to vigorous and idealised manhood are substantially removed from boys' fiction by the end of the century, and when they do appear, are attributed exclusively to 'vile' boys.

There are a number of factors which help to explain why it seems to have been perceived as necessary to encourage the next generation of men to adhere to new, more rigid and aggressive notions of masculinity. This encouragement took many forms, but probably none was more pronounced or effective than the boys' story. This is in part because children's literature had an established tradition of didacticism which made it a suitable vehicle for the transmission of values from one generation to the next. The didacticism of juvenile publishing was made (and remains) more effective by the increased emphasis on the education of children during this period, for childhood and adolescence make up the time of maximum learning – including the learning of values, behaviour and structures which are intended to be permanent.[3] Edward Salmon articulated this function of juvenile literature in *Juvenile Literature as it is*, telling those who would select from the suddenly abundant publishers' lists that it was impossible to overrate their importance for the national character and culture.[4]

One reason for the efficacy of the boys' story in promoting a new, more manly image of masculinity is that such stories converted social and economic pressures on young men into models capable of imitation and goals which seemed both desirable and attainable. Most important of all for adolescent readers, these stories helped to minimise conflict at a time when boys were likely to be highly concerned with sexuality. The boys' story of late-Victorian and Edwardian England is specifically directed at the audience of newly discovered adolescent youth. The concept of adolescence itself was new to the nineteenth century – a product of prosperity, leisure, prolonged education and the bourgeois household, and it seems likely that recognition of the transitional stage between childhood and maturity brought with it understanding that sexual identities are not straightforward and permanent. The fact that in fiction for boys social definitions of masculinity were reinforced through quintessentially male heroes and their exploits may be indicative of a new awareness that there could be problems involved in assuming masculine identity, and if problems, also failures.[5]

To clarify further the issue of sexual difference for boy readers, masculinity in these works is presented as the polar opposite of femininity. This meant that acceptably masculine behaviour in male characters could not include any characteristics associated with femininity. In this way boys' fiction provided a coherent, exclusively masculine subject position for its readers. The effect of constantly reinforcing this position was not only to define manliness, but to produce a reader who accepted the definition for, 'the relationship between symbol and symbolised is not only referential, does not simply describe, but is productive, that is, it creates.'[6]

One element which contributed to the initiation and perpetuation of changes to the existing definition of masculinity was the check to the economic boom. The worsening financial situation highlighted men's role as principal wage-earners and provided a context in which masculinity could be called into question. One consequence of this was a reaction against women in the work-force. As jobs became more scarce, working women, always a source of cheap labour, began to be valued less for the supplements they provided to family incomes and increasingly regarded as threatening. Men did not want to compete for jobs with women, for this would have had the combined effects of depressing wages and lowering occupational status. There thus came pressure to declare certain kinds of work masculine preserves. These invariably were classed as superior to work carried out by women and were better paid. The effect of such polarisation was twofold. It further devalued women's work (a process exacerbated by the complementary pressure to foreground new definitions of femininity and respectability which discouraged women from taking up work at all) and, in tandem with the resulting retreat into the home on the part of women, made a connection between masculinity and a man's ability to support his wife and family.[7]

A second, similar, factor which may have stimulated changes to the image of masculinity came from the movement to attain higher education for women – a further intrusion into what had been an all-male preserve. The early feminists' increasingly public and vociferous dissatisfaction with the positions and possibilities open to them undoubtedly generated unease. Attempts to redefine femininity were inevitably interpreted as assaults on masculine privilege and as affecting masculinity itself and gave rise to vigorous defences of the male position which took the form of attempts to demonstrate (through arguments based on the Bible, biology, medical evidence and historical precedent) male superiority and female inferiority. Challenges to the existing social order were thus construed as attacks on masculinity and generated a multiplicity of discourses with which to defend it and at the same time ensure the continuation of the patriarchal system.

At a more individual level, it is useful to note that it was during the nineteenth century that the absentee father (which Chodorow cites as a significant factor in the problematising of masculinity in modern society) became the norm. Movement away from the land, increased industrialisation and, for the middle classes the arrival of commuting as a regular feature of bourgeois life, meant that fathers were away from home more than before and work was generally less integrated in family life. Fathers became less known, more distant and increasingly associated with the outside world rather than with the home. As a consequence, there was a lack of male role models and the insistently masculine heroes of boys' fiction can be construed as filling this need for boys whose lives were otherwise predominantly controlled by women before and outside school.

During the nineteenth century sex was empowered with its present ability to define a person socially and morally.[8] The major social changes which accelerated throughout the last century gave rise to a socially constructed definition of normal sexuality used to control women and the working class.[9] Because this definition originated in and promoted a patriarchal structure, it is understandable that the implications for men are seen as less radical, as indeed they were. They are, nevertheless, significant – not only for understanding the subsequent shape of acceptable masculinity, but for exposing the impact on women of revisions in notions of masculinity, and on similarly structured power relations. The desire to instruct boys in masculinity, which is evident in the sector of juvenile publishing directed at them, is important for what it indicates about the changing attitude to notions of sexual difference. It seems likely that when the specific factors outlined above are added to the possibilities of major structural changes in social organisation associated with increased education and an expanding publishing industry, many of the ideological guys which for so long had secured definitions of masculinity and femininity were stretched to breaking point. They needed to be refurbished, and an obvious way of doing this was to accentuate differences. The privileged discourse of education, which had traditionally been the hallmark of a masculine élite, provided the basic material out of which was generated a more vigorously 'masculine' discourse. Furthermore, the shift from a general notion of masculinity, which could include affective qualities and such 'feminine' features as self-sacrifice, to a definition of masculinity which not only eliminates these qualities but also lays down strict guidelines about appropriate behaviour, must be significant.

The premises upon which patriarchy is founded were, in late-Victorian and Edwardian England, threatened not only by essentially external factors such as these, but also internally through conspicuous failures which questioned men's fitness for the position they held. For much of the Queen's reign, the Empire had generated a continuous and accelerating demand for armies and administrators. This gave rise to the proliferation of public schools for boys of the middle and lower-middle classes who aspired to military or civil service careers. Maturity for such boys basically meant moving from one all-male environment to another. While perhaps not consciously fostering misogyny, such institutions created an ethos which valued male friendships, interests and attributes above all things female. Rather than reviling women, they excluded them entirely or made them so marginal as to render them superfluous. This atmosphere was mirrored in the easy assumption of superiority and confidence exuded in the imaging of masculinity in early fiction for boys. By the end of the century, the naturalness of this posture was replaced by shrill insistence. It was at first as if the once flawless literary looking-glass had become a distorting mirror. If the new reflection it produced was more perfect than before, however, it was none the less a distortion, for the subject had begun to corrode. Great efforts had to be made to revitalise the masculine image; this was achieved by representing masculinity itself.

The accepted social definition of masculinity had not so much changed as been subjected to a regimen designed to build up and burnish the image of British manhood, particularly that put before the nation's youth, and in the process stripped of any extraneous or questionable attributes. Qualities such as loyalty, stoicism, courage, resourcefulness, athleticism and perhaps above all the ability to have the confidence and courage necessary to act as an individual, all of which characterise the new 'muscular' ideal in fiction for boys, were present in earlier works. The difference in the new presentation is one of intensity and focus. Where in early stories for boys failures in any of these areas would result in moral decline or the ruination of a scheme, they did not cast aspirations on a character's masculinity. He might be an impoverished human being, but notions of sexual difference are given and accepted in a casual way. Thus Farrar's Eric is presented as something of an aesthete and a coward (he is afraid to fight the school bully and his father has to do this for him), but even so, his masculinity is never in doubt. [10] This acceptance enables the earlier boys' fiction to include emotional displays and a strong sense of affective relationships which is quite different from the restrained co-operation of later works. The closing passages of *Tom Brown* provide an excellent example of qualities present in early examples of the genre but eradicated by the end of the century.

From the moment he learns of the Doctor's death, Tom is visibly moved. Upon entering the chapel where the Doctor is buried, he is overcome with emotion. Grief gives way to epiphany as memories call up love for all his old schoolmates with whom he is joined in sorrow. The text closes with a celebration of relationships: human and divine.

> Here let us leave him – where better . . . than at the altar, before which he had first caught a glimpse of the glory of his birthright, and felt the drawing of the bond which links all living souls together in one brotherhood. . . . And let us not be hard on him, if at that moment his soul is fuller of the tomb and him who lies there, than of the altar and Him of whom it speaks. . . . For it is only through our mysterious human relationships, through the love and tenderness and purity of mothers, and sisters, and wives, through the strength and courage and wisdom of fathers, and brothers, and teachers, that we can come to the knowledge of Him, in whom alone the love, and the tenderness, and the purity, and the strength, and the courage, and the wisdom of all these dwell for ever and ever in perfect fullness.

Compare these sentiments with those in Kipling's *Stalky & Co.* (1899), which a contemporary reviewer praised for the way it captures the essence of British boyhood including, 'the abhorrence of English boys – and for that matter, of English men – of having their sacred feelings referred to in public'.[11]

The key to this shift from casual, expansive images of masculinity to a uniform definition which is prescriptive and vigorously insisted upon seems to lie in the Empire. Once a source of pride, secure jobs, ready markets, cheap imports, and, above all, a perfect platform on which British soldiers could display their skills, the imperial play was threatening to close. It seemed the actors were forgetting lines, roles and even plots!

The Boer War epitomised British incompetence abroad – administrative and martial. And in exact proportion to the level of failure arose a rhetoric of jingoistic patriotism which proclaimed British as best. This trend was particularly evident in fiction for boys. Even such anti-heroes as Jack Harkaway (created by Bracebridge Hemyng for *Boys of England* in 1871) were reformed. Harkaway not only lost such unmanly characteristics as avoiding punishment, fighting unfairly, and kissing girls, but became the quintessential patriot.[12] The increase in the imperial theme in books and periodicals for boys at this time was 'presented in such a way as to inspire confidence and devotion'.[13] There was also a tendency in boys' fiction of the 1880s and 1890s to recreate the glories of England's past and to see them as the fruits of heroic deeds by men of action.[14]

Beneath the surface, however, unease was gathering. Had British boys become soft? Were the existing methods of education and training not fitting them for their required duties? Was modern youth lacking some quality possessed by the empire builders of the past? Were men less manly? After the débâcle at Mafeking (1900), anxiety about the next generation of men reached its peak. (Reed's *The Fifth Form at St Dominic's* (1881) seems to anticipate this trend for its final chapter, 'Good-bye to St Dominic's', reads like the obituary of an era. The giants of the fifth and sixth forms, whose deeds comprise most of the book, are legends and only recalled in the shapes of younger brothers or special pets left behind. More importantly, the lower forms have degenerated from the motley enough factions of the fourth juniors, known to readers as the Tadpoles and Guinea-pigs, to those styling themselves as the Buttercups and Daisies!) New publications, entirely devoted to inspiring boys with the need to defend their imperial heritage, proliferated. Magazines such as *Boys of Our Empire* (1900–3), *Chums* (1892–1934), and *The Captain* (1899–1924) chronicled the, usually imaginary, exploits of brave young Britons defending and enlarging Her Majesty's possessions. In tandem with such publications arose a number of military-style boys' movements: the Boys' Brigade (1883), the Boys' Empire League (1900), the Church Lads' Brigade (1891), the Lads' Drill Association (1899) and the Boy Scouts (1907). These groups were intended to improve fitness and discipline and raise morale. Their shared goal was to inspire each boy, 'by some direct effort, to make himself a fit and worthy representative of the British race'.[15]

The juvenile publishing industry found the interest in rearing a new breed of more masculine boys made for good business. It produced not only periodicals and similarly themed books of war-time adventures, but also found a market in nostalgia for boyhood and an all-male world which gave rise to a literature intended to be shared by men and boys. As Musgrave points out in his study of the boys' school story, the middle-class men who ran the publishing businesses had sound financial and social reasons for revitalising the male image and maintaining the patriarchal system under which they had flourished.[16]

Thus, at the time when publishing for juveniles was becoming established – its foundations being laid and successful formulae, conventions, features, styles and characters being bottled and preserved – economic pressures, challenges from women and notable failures in exclusively male arenas seem to have initiated a collective recognition of the need to instruct boys in a particular code of masculinity. This entailed the repression and disparagement of emotions, gestures and attitudes which might be construed as feminine, and the magnification of attributes deemed masculine. The heroes of boys' fiction became manlier than manly: braver, stronger, more loyal, more patriotic, more cunning, more masterful and more reticent than ever before.

A consequence of this determination to produce more masculine boys is a decidedly anti-intellectual strain in their fiction: muscle and morality are celebrated over intelligence and inspiration. Accordingly, sporting events or other similar occasions (spontaneous races, games, fights, or rescues) received considerable attention and encouraged boys to see themselves, their trials, opportunities and triumphs, as belonging to a public sphere of action rather than taking place internally. This tendency is epitomised in the poems of Sir Henry Newbolt typified by his '*Vitae Lampada*'.

> There's a breathless hush in the Close tonight –
> Ten to make and the match to win –
> A bumping pitch and a blinding light,
> An hour to play and the last man in.

> And it's not for the sake of a ribboned coat,
> Or the selfish hope of a season's fame,
> But his Captain's hand on his shoulder smote –
> 'Play up! play up! and play the game!'

If it is accepted that the activity of reading is part of the process of forming a sexual identity, then the standardisation of representations of masculinity and the kind of language boys are guided to acquire through literature must be seen as noteworthy. Howarth's study of heroes in popular fiction (1973) sees Newbolt's works not only as encapsulating the masculine ideal as it had evolved in the second half of the last century, but also as profoundly influencing representations of masculinity in popular fiction. As evidence that literary representations do affect social behaviour, Howarth cites the influence of Talbot Baines Reed's brand of school story on the appearance of public school boys (the dates he gives provide further evidence for a shift to more rigorous notions of masculinity after the Boer War). He writes:

> In presenting heroes who constantly conform to type, popular school stories may have reflected a tendency towards increased standardisation in the public school product himself. In 1912 Arthur Ponsonby, in his book *The Decline of the Aristocracy*, wrote that stereotyping was 'perhaps the strongest indictment that has to be brought against our Public Schools'. In illustration of this he contrasted group photographs taken at schools in the 1860s and 1870s in which there had been considerable variety in individuality of appearance, with the general conformity to type in comparable photographs forty to fifty years later. It is also likely that Reed and his successors in their very popularity contributed to this standardisation.[17]

A second feature of this new preoccupation with providing muscle-bound images of masculinity is the monothematic nature of the fantasy material it produces. Freud has taught us that sexuality is nowhere more active than at the level of fantasy.[18] In fiction for boys the material for fantasy is severely limited. Heroes and exploits follow similar patterns, whatever the circumstances. The only real material for fantasy is the ultramasculine hero, and hero worship is the intended goal.[19] This is true even of those works in which adults return to childhood scenarios. If childhood is the time in which the image of the self is formed, there is a steady pressure in boys' fiction to present and represent boyhood and nascent masculinity as mutually inclusive and univalent. The language used, like the images presented, is consistently unambiguous.

During the last century definitions of appropriate sexual behaviour – that is behaviour which reproduced and supported the bourgeois nuclear family (central both to industrial capitalism and to patriarchy) came to prominence as did means of monitoring and regulating unacceptable behaviour.[20] Boys' literature is a product of these controls. It refuses to incorporate any ambivalent sexual models or to explore problems surrounding sexual difference in content or language. Appropriate models of masculinity and femininity are promoted vigorously and are presented as unproblematic. Perversion is denied through the exclusion of specific references and through the implication that to be other than the ideal is to be not only despicable, but also incapacitated. Through these means boys' fiction attempts to ensure that the kind of sexuality to which its readers aspire is that which most adults find comfortable – heterosexual love is the only possible outcome of maturity. Such insistence and significant silences need always to be understood as part of the proliferation of discourses about sexuality which were generated in the nineteenth century and which would indicate that masculine sexuality was in fact not regarded as the straightforward issue it appears.[21]

Thus, through a combination of specific circumstances and changing social patterns, boys' reading began to play a significant part in defining and instilling acceptable images of the kind valued in male-dominated societies. Fiction for boys perpetuated processes of separation and recognition of difference from the mother begun in infancy, and extolled an ethic of work, endeavour and mastery over social and cultural inferiors, and over women. The process was continued by boys' being discouraged from developing a taste for literature, and being encouraged to read non-fiction.[22] This served to limit the material for fantasy, to inhibit in boys the passive and dependent posture of the heavy reader of fiction, and discouraged linguistic experimentation which might undermine a coherent sense of the masculine self. Power was presented as the ability to act, to use language decisively and to contain emotion. The boy reader was guided into a position which was likely to make him support the existing social structure, the hierarchies and legislation which maintained it, and the control of which was shown to be his inheritance. It seems in fact that juvenile books as a whole, and books for boys in particular, have helped to perpetuate male dominance and the reproduction of notions of sexual difference which entitle boys to public privileges, but do so at the expense of their ability to form affective relationships. The effect this has on girls and women and their reading habits forms the basis of Chapter 5. The next chapter considers in detail some of the most popular turn-of-the-century publications for boys and the men who produced them.

Chapter 4

Bracing, bold and British: G. A. Henty, Talbot Baines Reed and the **Boy's Own Paper**

There was nothing namby-pamby in Henty's writings, for his adolescent characters are not so much boys as men, saving in this, that he kept them to boy life, and never made his works sickly by the introduction of what an effeminate writer would term the tender passion.

(G. Manville Fenn's *George Alfred Henty: The story of an active life*, 1907, p. 321)

Morally, the book is everything that could be desired, setting before the boys a bright and bracing ideal of the English gentleman.

(from a review of Henty's *By Sheer Pluck* in *The Christian Leader*, 1889)

The significance of G. A. Henty (1839–1902) and Talbot Baines Reed (1852–93) to the development of the two major genres within boys' fiction is incontestable. *The Oxford Companion to Children's Literature* describes Henty as the 'British writer of the most popular and enduring of the late-nineteenth century adventure stories for boys'; the same volume says of Reed that he, 'more than any other writer was responsible for establishing the school story as a genre popular enough to rival the adventure story in sales and readership'. The debt owed by generations of British boys to these writers is consistently underlined in reviews, advertisements, biographies, and criticisms from the last century to the present day.[1]

As together their work comprises a huge body of the most popular and long-lived of late-Victorian and Edwardian boys' stories produced in both serial and book form, Henty and Reed seemed the obvious pair from whose work to derive and illustrate general conclusions about boys' fiction of this period. The apparently seamless connection between life and work, the lack of contradiction, hesitancy, or tension available in biographies or accounts of their working methods and the legendary quality which characterises studies about both men in fact make it difficult to deal with them as individuals. There is a constant pressure to regard them as phenomena, and to accept without question the consistency between glossy and attractive covers and the contents of both men and their books.

This pressure was not unique to Henty and Reed. Similar magnifications and idealisations surrounded many of the most prominent nineteenth-century writers for boys (for instance R. M. Ballantyne, Captain Marryat, W. E. Johns and Kipling). The creation of such 'giants' during an age of exploration and colonial power is not, perhaps, unexpected. However, the emotional dynamic behind the public presentation of these writers is far from simple, as becomes evident from considering the images of Henty and Reed. Because so much biographical material about both writers is available elsewhere, I have kept such information to a minimum, concentrating instead on the interpretation and reception of the men and their writing.[2]

Writers and role models

There evidently existed a compulsion to turn Henty and Reed (and no doubt many other men behind boys' fiction) into masculine ideals in the mould of their time. Just as boys' fiction seems to have been bent on minimising ambiguity and emotional exploration while promoting clearly defined – even heightened – images and ambitions deemed appropriately masculine, so there appears to have been a collective need to make its authors paradigms for their creations:

> Life was uncomplicated for Henty, and it held few mysteries. The difference between right and wrong, virtue and vice was always clearly discernable . . . Henty's own adventure career, his large frame and bearded face, personified the self-confidence of late Victorian England. . . . His importance lies . . . in the extent to which he heightened and tinted an already existing stereotype and so coloured the attitudes and opinions of future generations.[3]

The pressure to idealise these men who wielded such influence over their boy readers may be interpreted as a reflection of the unease generated by widespread social change and disruption of tradition. The setting up of Henty and Reed as public figures can usefully be understood as an example of 'positive stereotyping'. In his history of the stereotype, Sander L. Gilman (1985) concludes that all stereotypes are used to help preserve a sense of control and a sense of self in the face of instabilities.

> When . . . the sense of order and control undergoes stress, when doubt is cast on the self's ability to control the internalised world that it has created for itself, an anxiety appears which mirrors the earlier affective colouring of the period of individuation. We project that anxiety onto the Other, externalising our loss of control. The Other is thus stereotyped, labelled with a set of signs paralleling (or mirroring) our loss of control. The Other is invested with all of the qualities of the 'bad' or the 'good'.[4]

Gilman identifies two kinds of stereotype – the bad (what we fear to become) and the good (what we fear we will fail to achieve) – but really develops only the function of negative stereotypes as 'images that demean, and by demeaning, control'.[5] For sexual stereotyping, therefore, he is concerned almost exclusively with that surrounding women. It seems equally important to look at the reverse – the positive stereotyping of masculinity – both as a phenomenon in itself and as a reaction to the negative stereotyping developing around passionate women. Both are part of the tendency, which increased throughout the nineteenth century, to use the sexual as a means of defining normal and pathological individuals. The heightening of gender codes, as with those of class, can be understood in part as a reaction to the social upheavals which came with industrialisation, urbanisation and affluence. They are a way of insisting upon stability and forcing links with a notion of past proprieties which it was feared were being effaced.

The polarisation of good and bad, normal and abnormal is particularly pronounced in juvenile publications, in which all subjects are necessarily treated as simply and unambiguously as possible. Moreover, such fiction provides an obvious medium for instructing the young reader in socially desirable behaviour. Thus, while sexual deviance is given no place in the juvenile fiction of this period, the insistence on the normal is so inflated as to be obsessive. Certainly to the present-day reader this exaggerated concern with 'normal' sexuality frequently registers as a dialectic with the abnormal which is so aggressively excluded.

The inscription of supernormal, idealised masculinity in books for boys, while undoubtedly intended to provide role models to instruct boys in manly ways, can nevertheless be understood as existing more for the ease of the adults who wrote, purchased, recommended and frequently read such works, than for the 'intended' audience. Such positive stereotyping would have helped to minimise concern about the pace and types of change taking place socially which inevitably added a new dimension to the differences between adult and child. Gilman postulates that the stereotype is in fact a peculiarly adult way of dealing with anxiety:

> The deep structure of the stereotype reappears [in the sense that it is part of the process of differentiating self from other begun by the child] in the adult as a response to anxiety, having its roots in the potential disintegration of the mental representatives the individual has created and internalised.[6]

In juvenile fiction, the use of positive stereotyping to allay adult anxieties was linked to questions of address, sexuality, and images of childhood and the child reader. It provided an appealing short cut which bypassed all of these dubious regions. The idealised images of masculinity and femininity in these books preserved notions of childhood innocence and instructed young readers in what was socially acceptable without introducing troublings of sexuality. Children's sexuality was, and is, problematic – an area of taboo – and as such was incorporated in discourses of perversion. Regarded as sexual precocity, it challenges prevailing (adult) definitions of normality.[7] It also destroys the child as the symbol of purity and link with a utopianised past, both of which functions were

67

being increasingly elaborated in Victorian/Edwardian art and letters. Indeed, when Henty once had a hero kiss his sweetheart, he was reproved by a clergyman and, apparently on the strength of this single objection, dispensed with all such incidents in perpetuity.[8] That he was conscious of the need to keep sexuality from tainting his role models is further evidenced by the exclusion of Nelson from the British heroes whose lives he so frequently used as the basis for historical books. Nelson (presumably because of his attachment to Lady Hamilton) was deemed too 'Latin' to make a suitable subject.[9]

The move from characters to authors is not vast – the two are frequently bound up and confused in the reader's mind. Those who deal with young people in any capacity are, rightly or wrongly, generally expected to be exemplary. It is therefore not surprising that men with the proven influence over their youthful readership commanded by Henty and Reed were expected not only to provide patterns in their books, but also to *be* patterns. The pressure to personify the masculine ideal must have been particularly strong at a time when, as we have seen, there were conspicuous failures in and challenges to traditional male arenas. Women, both perforce and voluntarily, were agitating for revisions to definitions of femininity and in the process beginning to question the foundations of male supremacy. It is not surprising, then, that these two men seem not just to have been made the appointed guardians of the morals and future of the next generation, but also to have perceived themselves as embodying late-Victorian values. They became archetypal patriarchs, filling the gaps in households where fathers were often absent. At the same time, they attempted through their books to give birth in the only conceivable male way – by begetting clones capable of proving that Britannia still ruled the waves.

Henty

Henty began his writing career as a war correspondent when posted to the Crimea. He said that a writer such as himself should be capable of supporting hardships and fatigues; . . . should possess a certain amount of pluck, a good seat in the saddle such as would enable him to manage any mount whose services he could command; and lastly . . . he should have the manners of a gentleman and the knack of getting on with all sorts and conditions of men.[10]

These are precisely the qualities he seeks to instil in the 'lads' to whom he addressed his books. Indeed, he offers himself as a template for his readers, for the Henty heroes on whom boys were to model themselves shared striking similarities with their creator. Most are introduced as small, cheerful, industrious, witty and, above all, *plucky* boys who get themselves swept up in military careers. In the course of their adventures, these youths acquire stature, status and fortunes. This progress mirrors Henty's own. He grew from a puny stripling into a massive man. He won his fortune and reputation by rubbing along in all kinds of circumstances, with all types of men. Industrious and always prepared to put himself in dangerous situations, Henty endured a variety of physical hardships and survived an impressive number of campaigns (though not in active service). It seems he was always ready to impose his authority on others and to back up threats with his fists. Just as Henty's plucky heroes prove themselves able to whip at least twice their number of foreigners and cads, so Henty maintained that a 'muscular and athletic English gentleman' was capable of administering a 'thoroughly sound and manly thrashing' to disorderly ruffians.[11] In doing so he believed he won both respect and affection.

The merging of fact and fiction continued. Like his young heroes, Henty was present at significant military and historic moments. He was an army administrator in the Crimea and during the Austro-Italian campaign; as a foreign correspondent he covered Garibaldi's campaign in Italy, the opening of the Suez canal, the Paris Commune, the Ashanti campaign and the Prince of Wales's tour of India. The last major incident he covered involved following the Turks into Servia in 1876.[12]

Henty's boys-who-will-be-heroes are generally introduced

on the point of leaving school, where their academic careers have been less than brilliant. Sport and the great outdoors have been their training grounds, for it quickly becomes clear that the books are grounded in the belief that it is through achieving physical prowess and exercising his courage that a boy becomes a man. Skills such as boxing, shooting and sailing are understood to sharpen the wits more effectively than studying the subjects likely to make up the syllabus for most middle-class boys. Thus when the nascent hero embarks on his career, his failings in Latin are more of a commendation than a handicap, as Charlie Marryat discovers in *With Clive in India* (1884). When interviewing Charlie his prospective Commander declares:

> 'Give me a lad with pluck and spirit, and I don't care a snap of my fingers whether he can construe Euripides or solve a problem in higher mathematics. What we want for India are men who can ride and shoot, who are ready at any moment to start on a hundred mile journey on horseback, who will scale a hill fort with a handful of men or with half a dozen Sowars tackle a dacoit and his band. What do the natives care for our learning? It is pluck and fighting power that have made us their masters.'   (p. 23)

The complete Henty bibliography contains approximately 220 pieces, 90 of which are boys' adventure stories.[13] Henty dictated his stories to an amanuensis. The two devised a streamlined system which enabled them to complete a book in as few as twenty days once the actual writing process had begun. An important element in the hugely successful Henty formula is the imparting of detailed information about historical periods and military campaigns. Much of this material he lifted more or less verbatim from other sources, so that at times his 'dictation' seems to have consisted of reading aloud from works such as Sir William Napier's *History of the War in the Peninsula*.[14] This practice, together with the reliance on dictation and the speed at which the pair worked, resulted in writing which was extremely uneven. An examination of his books shows them to be montages, in which the different pieces are clearly separate. Nevertheless, Henty's skill at episodic narrative was such that his popularity was phenomenal and even the most detailed history lessons sandwiched between events seem to have been happily ingested by his young readers. Henty's heroes have lives which are remarkably clear cut from start to finish. From poor but genteel beginnings they rise to squiredom, with no impediments to their progress once it has begun. There are no real villains in Henty books (only enemies who are respected for their military prowess which makes them worthy adversaries) and very few failures. Virtue and industry are instantly and publicly recognised and rewarded, and Henty's heroes never have to overcome emotional problems in order to gain their objectives. Their lives are free from moral conflict; difficulties always take the form of physical hardships which can be overcome and/or endured. Significantly, these young men have no problems in communicating with people of any age, sex, or station. Beardless youths who have never seen a battle advise admirals and generals, who invariably listen carefully and act upon what they have heard. Indeed, it is sometimes necessary for the hero to remind his seniors of his inexperience, as happens in *Held Fast for England* (1892). After capturing an enemy vessel, seventeen-year-old civilian Bob Repton is told by the Captain of the ship on which he is a passenger to take command of his prize. Bob replies, 'It was all very well getting on board and knocking down the crew, but when it comes to sailing her, it is perfectly ridiculous my giving orders when the men know that I don't know anything about it.' The Captain responds, 'The men know you have plenty of pluck, Bob, and they know that it was entirely due to your swimming off to that Spanish ship that we escaped from being captured before, and they will obey you willingly as far as you can give them orders.' (p. 223)

What is left out of Henty's books is any sense of the self as problematic. There is no attempt to render interior monologue, personal struggle or unconscious motivation. The tales are told in the third person by an omniscient narrator. The characters are essentially two-dimensional. With the possible exception of Jack Simpson in *Facing Death* (1882), they exhibit no interest in themselves further than becoming successful in order to support dependent relations and to take on civic responsibilities. There is no doubt, contradiction or hesitation to provide tension; nor is there any romantic interest with which to introduce speculation about how the character is perceived or acts outside his professional career. The interest comes entirely from the action, all of which takes place in the domain Ruskin delineated as man's province.

Reed

While structurally very similar to Henty's, the work of Talbot Baines Reed incorporates many of the elements which Henty's formula so scrupulously avoided. This may be because there was a greater disparity between Reed's background and achievements and those of the heroes he created than was the case for Henty. Reed never attended a school like those about which he wrote and, though an excellent athlete, most of his feats, and all of his adventures, took place behind a desk.

Reed's young heroes lived the same kind of full and active lives that he had as a boy. Like Henty, Reed seems to have been convinced that his was the right way of going about becoming a man, and to have modelled his characters accordingly, in the belief that his readers would follow their examples. Reed was a swimmer and belonged to the London Rifle Brigade; his heroes tended to be equally good sportsmen. Jim Halliday, one of the young men whose story is recounted in *The Adventures of a Three-Guinea Watch* (1880), is described as 'a strapping youth', 'a good bat, a famous boxer, a desperate man in a football scrimmage, and a splendid oar' (p. 31). In *The Fifth Form at St. Dominic's* (1881–2), three of the boys battle with the landlord of the local inn and his cronies and win. This is a clear example of Reed's view of the world where, 'A pair of well-trained athletic schoolboys, with a plucky youngster to help them, are a match any day for twice the number of half tipsy cads.' (p. 118)

The similarities in tone and ideal with those encountered in Henty's books is obvious in these passages, but unlike Henty,

Reed addressed himself in addition to the problems of those boys who were deficient in some way. Often this was done by pairing a strong, sound, quick character with one who is weak or in some way handicapped. While Henty's books consistently plot the rise of their heroes as they experience adventures and trials in which their courage and physical prowess are enabled to shine, the characters in the books of Reed have less incontrovertibly successful careers. Each is presented with some kind of trial of character which frequently corrects faults and ultimately proves him free from the taints of the sneak, the duffer, the bully and other of the ungentlemanly traits identified, described and lampooned for his readers.

Henty's heroes are essentially the same at the opening of their stories as they are at the conclusion. When the reader is introduced to them these boys are already known for their physical prowess, courage and ability to get along with others. Capitalising on such innate qualities – which are never the source of envy – once launched on the world they rapidly win respect. Good health, a sound constitution, courage and wit ensure success. After each bold deed comes recognition and reward, so young midshipmen and privates rapidly ascend the ladder of command. The financial gains and accompanying security with which Henty rewards his heroes have been the goal all along. While his young men are quite clearly gentlemen by nature (and frequently by birth as well), they are equally consistently of humble means. This combination accounts for their positions (usually they begin active service as junior officers) and success. Furthermore, when character and ability are rewarded, the youths' pedigrees ensure that there is no problem of class when they set up genteel establishments.

By contrast, Reed's characters have much less straight-forwardly brilliant careers (though they are no less middle-class in origin and concern). There are no sieges, Black Holes, or battles to endure; their sufferings are of a different sort. For instance, in *The Fifth Form at St. Dominic's*, Oliver Greenfield is wrongly accused of stealing an exam paper and made an outcast at the school. His honesty, courage and steadfast nature throughout the ordeal not only result in total vindication, but also steady his younger brother. Through Oliver's example, Greenfield minor learns to withstand the ill winds of temptation emanating from the Cockchafer Inn. The lack of such a positive influence is bemoaned by the weak and unfortunate Loman, whose career (as his name indicates) descends from the lofty heights of monitor to the depths of expulsion.

This straightforward example of the strong and able bringing about the reform of their lesser companions is repeated in *Tom, Dick and Harry* (1892), in which the well-intentioned but foolish and impressionable Tom is befriended by a variety of steady fellows whose efforts on his behalf transform him from idle duffer to the top of his form. In the process, Tom inadvertently galvanises his entire house, raising it from the worst in the school to the best. The most elaborate use of this opposition is made in *The Adventures of a Three-Guinea Watch*.

In this story Reed is at pains to show that weakness comes in many forms. The watch's first owner, Charlie Newcome, is possessed of all the qualities which graced the proper British schoolboy. His successors, however, are less fortunate. Upon receiving a new gold repeater, Charlie bequeaths the silver three-guinea watch given to him by his father on his first day of school to his friend, Tom Drift. Drift, when first introduced to the reader, is an unlikely companion for so shining a boy. Through Charlie's persistence he becomes a hard-working and likeable young man. Away from school and his friend's good influence, however, Tom literally drifts from his regular habits and industrious ways. Beginning with music halls and novel reading, he rapidly descends to gambling, drinking and the things which attend them until, so debauched that he is expelled from medical school, he is rejected by society and separated from all that had been good in his life. At this point Drift pawns the watch which, never being redeemed, is later sold. In this way it comes into the possession of George Reader. This young man's weakness is quite the reverse of Tom Drift's. A brilliant scholar from a poor family, he wins a scholarship to Oxford. There he proceeds to burn himself out through sheer hard work and the refusal to develop other aspects of his personality. Though he achieves astonishingly fine examination results, he is too weak to enjoy his triumph, and dies, thus leaving unfulfilled all of the promise he and others had hoped he would give to enrich the world.

Though George Reader's weakness proves fatal, Tom Drift is given a second chance. An old schoolmate discovers him in prison and, through the agency of the watch, helps him to turn again to a worthwhile life and resume his medical studies. This leads to the last major incident in the book in which surgeon Drift appears on the battlefield and saves Charlie Newcome's life by removing a bullet which had lodged in his chest.

Reed repeatedly stresses that gifts and abilities are of less importance than basic character and a healthy, disciplined lifestyle. His brightest young men are often the quickest to succumb to temptation and squander their talents. Those who, like Reed himself, combine the Smilesian qualities of industry, self-discipline and honesty with active outdoor pursuits are rewarded with full and satisfying lives. The lessons he taught, then, were similar to Henty's, but operated in a different milieu and he attempted to deal with at least some of the problems likely to be encountered by his young readers.

Another way in which the works of the two men are noticeably different is in their treatment of issues surrounding masculinity and femininity. This difference can in part be considered a consequence of the fact that they worked in different genres. Thus Henty, who adheres firmly to the dictates and conventions of the adventure story, invariably relies on the heightened presentation of masculinity that such stories seem to require. The adventure genre does not ask that the world be shown in microcosm; neither is there any structural value in exploring affective relationships or emotional problems. By working within the adventure convention, Henty was able legitimately to exclude precisely these areas from his work and to concentrate instead on detailing the characteristics which make his heroes embodiments of the masculine ideal. By implication, a healthy boy, and one who succeeds in the world, is not introspective, tender, or compassionate to any notable degree.

No matter the horrors witnessed, there is no indication that any of Henty's heroes is in the least affected by them. Instead, each incident is seen as experience which will help further a career. As part of a profile of a society which was consistently attempting to teach a particular and pronounced notion of masculinity, this fact becomes most interesting. Elaine Showalter's study of hysteria (*The Female Malady*, 1985) looks closely at the phenomenon known as 'shell shock' which affected large numbers of soldiers during and after the First World War. Shell shock, she concludes, was a form of male hysteria – a reaction against the enormous pressures to conform to an exaggerated model of masculinity experienced by soldiers in a time of conflict. The pressures were increased not only through the atmosphere engendered by the war, but by trends in Victorian psychiatry and society. By the time of the First World War, she suggests, 'manly' had come to mean, 'rational, not emotional; deliberate rather than impulsive'.[15] A mental breakdown of any kind was regarded as an affront to masculinity; particularly during a time of war such an affront was intolerable. The victims of shell shock were accordingly treated as pariahs – they were regarded as moral invalids and this treatment increased the anxiety they were feeling. Discouraged from articulating their feelings, soldiers found themselves in a position which Showalter identifies as essentially female – forced to give vent to their emotional problems through their bodies.

Henty, although living through the period in which these changes were taking place and a veteran of many campaigns, never gives any insight into this kind of reaction. His well-disciplined troops march to inevitable slaughter as eagerly and resolutely as to a possible victory. There is no instance of a soldier expressing discontent with the role expected of him. Masculinity is a given – an irrefutable quality – in Henty's heroes and the troops they lead. Perhaps as part of this determined assertion of the naturalness of masculinity, Henty also finds himself unable to question the virtues of experience and ageing. Maturity is presented only as the culmination of successful youth; experience does not involve sacrificing boyish qualities of innocence and vision, but realising and capitalising on innate abilities through industry and self-discipline.

Girls in a man's world

Possibly because he never admitted that boys could experience problems in becoming masculine, Henty was prepared to give to girls and women their portion of excitement and pluck. That he does so is probably also influenced by a variety of other, more immediate, pressures. First, it was an obvious marketing strategy. Girls were avid readers of Henty stories and corresponded enthusiastically with the author. Second, Henty was actually in the Crimea during the time that Florence Nightingale and her staff so effectively battled against administrative incompetence. Henty was affected personally, because his elder brother caught cholera as a result of inadequate and inappropriate provisions and planning. His admiration for Nightingale's achievements strengthened with every campaign on which he was in attendance, and he never let pass an opportunity to criticise the short-sighted, befuddled management of the British army. Such direct sympathy for Nightingale would only have coloured a more general impression of the shift taking place in attitudes towards women; not just as a result of social necessity at home, but also with a view to preparing those girls who were to be the future wives of men stationed in the far-flung corners of the Empire. Nightingale must be regarded as a major public face of the women who negotiated the conflicting demands arising from such situations. They needed to be feminine and yet able to withstand the physically demanding and politically precarious existence of pioneer women. Frequently in juvenile fiction such women are depicted professionally shooting a gang of bandits, only to swoon helplessly the moment the crisis is over.[16]

This yoking together of the feminine ideal with the vigour and capability required by the imperial helpmeet figures in several Henty stories. It is important to note that the work in which he most overtly lectures young men on the qualities of women restricts this praise to the preface and confines it to historical and military models. By contrast, in the text he describes a different kind of domestic, feminised, heroism. The text is *One of the 28th* (1890). In his preface Henty writes:

Boys are apt to think, mistakenly, that their sex has a monopoly of courage, but I believe that in moments of great peril, women are to the full as brave and collected as men. Indeed, my own somewhat extensive experience leads me to go even farther, and to assert that among a civil population, untrained to arms, the average woman is cooler and more courageous than the average man. Women are nervous about little matters; they may be frightened of a mouse or at a spider; but in the presence of real danger, when shells are bursting in the streets, and rifle bullets flying thickly, I have seen them standing knitting at their doors and talking to their friends across the street when not a single man was to be seen.   (p. v)

He goes on to say that women are better at enduring pain and that boys 'ought not to consider themselves superior in every way' (p. vi).

In *One of the 28th*, Henty provides little opportunity for observing the kind of courage he describes in the preface. The act of 'heroism' which he presents as comprising the interest of the story consists of the hero's mother disguising herself as a servant and searching a house in which she believes an ageing pair of sisters have hidden a will which would benefit her son. In this book, however, Henty does create the opportunity to contrast some of the conditioning to which boys and girls are subjected and their behaviour. He appears to conclude that in youth the differences between the sexes are minimal. This is shown through the character of Mable Withers. Mable is the daughter of a clergyman who is the close friend of Herbert Penfold. Penfold introduces her to the hero, Ralph Conway, for he plans to divide his fortune between the pair in the hope that they will one day marry. The difference between the boy and girl is captured in their use of language. Upon meeting Ralph, Mable tells him that she thinks he is 'nice'. The young man rejoins, 'I think you look jolly . . . and that's better than looking nice.' To which Mable replies, 'I think they mean the same thing . . . except that a girl says "nice" and a boy says "jolly". I like "jolly" best, only I get scolded when I use it.' (pp. 37–38) Thus Mable, whom Ralph finds remarkable for her naturalness and direct speech, is nevertheless conscious of constraints in her use of language to which boys are less subject.

Henty's view of young women seems to be loosely derived from Rousseau. He finds society impairs rather than improves the maiden, as Mr Penfold explains to Ralph.

> You see, Ralph, girls brought up in a town are naturally different to one like Mable. They go to school, and are taught to sit upright and to behave discreetly, and to be generally unnatural. Mable has been brought up at home, and allowed to do as she liked, and she has consequently grown up what nature intended her to be.   (p. 39)

The enigma of femininity is explored in no greater detail in *One of the 28th*. *A Soldier's Daughter* (1906), however, provides considerably more evidence that Henty felt the need to create a female character who fitted into the tumultuous worlds he described, yet was also unmistakeably a lady in the conventional sense. Such a combination was necessary to make a worthy match for his heroes. Henty creates his ideal woman by granting her a period of license prior to womanhood during which to act out her fantasies involving the possession of male power and freedom without being sexually compromised.

Although in *A Soldier's Daughter* Henty enables his heroine (and so, vicariously, his girl readers) temporarily to fulfil her desire to be a boy, the story in the end confirms the status quo in sexual relations. Despite the heroine's skill with a rifle and her speed of thought and speech when a military crisis comes, she soon feels inferior to the men. Feminine weaknesses regularly impede her masculine ambitions; her adventure is in fact a tempering process, preparing her to accept her role as a woman. Nevertheless, Henty does consider the fact that girls may have the desire to behave like boys and may be dissatisfied with the strictures laid upon them by society. However, even when in some senses dealing with girls' fantasies, Henty does not alter his story-telling technique to incorporate a vocabulary or structure which would facilitate examination of the self. The text progresses through action alone. Neither does he ever explore the reverse possibility – no Henty hero ever fantasises about being a girl, nor is he placed in the situation of the female. The same cannot be said of Reed.

Reed and Henty were much alike in their adherence to late-Victorian definitions of the manly man, yet before achieving this goal, some of Reed's characters are put in essentially feminine positions. This is most readily seen in *Tom, Dick and Harry*, when the foolish young Tom Jones is first sent to a girls' school to be crammed for Low Heath, and then promptly nicknamed Sarah by his house. Sarah's loquaciousness borders on sneaking; Sarah acts intuitively rather than rationally; Sarah is a dandy and a gossip (both failings identified with women); Sarah is slack at lessons and easily compromised. As the story unfolds, Tom tries to master Sarah. With the help of stolid Dicky Brown and the captain of the rugby team, some progress is made. Nevertheless, Sarah continues to cause trouble until one night she is carried from a burning building and confined to bed for several weeks. From bed Sarah, with Mrs Jones in attendance, gives tea parties. In this classically feminine position, Tom finally overcomes Sarah. After being pronounced well, he attends sports day – too weak to participate, but not too weak to be put in charge of a friend's riotous siblings. Instead of Sarah the nursemaid, who would have been isolated by her duties and would somehow have caused a catastrophe, it is Tom who takes charge of the irrepressible infants. His success with them marks the turning point in his career at school; he is now able to benefit from his efforts at reforming himself. Friends assist him in his task, which is completed with no untoward accidents. Moreover, his house, once the worst in the school, comes top in the games entirely thanks to Tom's suggestion that membership of the previously undisciplined Philosophers Club be based on achievement. The work ethic so introduced includes training (in secret) for sports day and leads to the glorious surprise victory. Although unable to represent his house in the games, Tom comes top of his form in the annual examinations and thus takes over presidency of the club for the following year, when he knows that he will return to Low Heath, not as a silly new boy, but as one of the school's established leaders and steady personalities.

Reed tended to attribute mildly feminine traits to his characters during an interlude when they were attempting to recover from some mistake in judgement. The feminine situation is in one sense a trial to be endured, and, in another, part of the healing process itself. In accordance with the nineteenth-century division of the sexes into separate spheres, the male, who is begrimed by the world, needs to be cleansed through the female. Rather than introducing women as agents of this redemption (though there are often female characters associated with the process), Reed has his characters take on the female role for themselves. That he does so may have less to do with a notion of the self, which potentially includes both masculine and feminine traits, than with his taking literally the belief that moral weakness as much as physical is unmanly; having done their penance and rid themselves of their failings, his boys mature into the masculine ideal.

It is important to note that at no time during these feminine periods do the young men question their manliness, nor does the language suggest any kind of emotional crisis. Though dealing with incidents which were more likely to occur for readers than those Henty describes, Reed's books continue to operate through action rather than emotional exploration. There is no introduction of problems in dealing with the world which cannot be overcome through industry and self-discipline. Both Reed and Henty are schooling their readers in ways to succeed in the world – which do not include questioning the way in which their readers perceive themselves. Equally, they avoid literary language and concentrate on imparting information and codes of behaviour through entertaining narratives. Their books are tailored to an audience being instructed in masculinity; reinforcing masculine stereotypes and discouraging the development of qualities such as sensitivity, nurturing and intuitiveness which were designated feminine.

Reed's and Henty's books are among those which have taken on high status within the juvenile canon. Now regarded principally as collector's items, for decades they belonged to an area of juvenile fiction which was read and praised by adults on the basis of content. Books for girls written by authors of equal popularity suffered precisely the opposite fate. They tended to be devalued in their day, and though now they are beginning to be collected as attractive period examples, they continue to be regarded as inferior to their male counterparts. Before shifting to publishing for girls, however, it is necessary to consider a publication which played a major role in developing fiction for boys in late-Victorian and Edwardian England: the *Boy's Own Paper*.

The Boy's Own Paper

The only real antidote for these poisonous sheets . . . is the *Boy's Own Paper*, because the *Boy's Own Paper* is the only first-class journal of its kind to find its way into the slums as well as into the best homes.

(Edward J. Salmon's *Juvenile Literature as it is*, 1888)

We certainly aim to keep the *Boy's Own Paper* far ahead, in point of real merit, of any of its competitors, though we fear that all boys have not gumption enough to appreciate the difference between journals merely filled with improbable stories written to order by people who have never seen, and probably know little or nothing about what they profess to describe; and a paper like our own, in which both writers and artists occupy the highest place in public estimation, and are recognised authorities on the subjects with which they respectively deal.

This claim was made in an early number (23 August, 1880) of the *Boy's Own Paper* by two of its guiding lights. Talbot Baines Reed's contributions of serialised fiction and shorter stories have already been discussed in some detail. His friend, George Andrew Hutchinson, with whom he collaborated on this pronouncement which featured in the correspondence section of the magazine, was officially recognised as the *BOP*'s principal editor in 1897. In fact, Hutchinson both conceived the characteristic and unexpectedly successful mixture of fiction, practical articles and lighter (but never entirely frivolous) features, and was its editor in all but name

from the time that the Religious Tract Society determined to
bring out a wholesome magazine for boys.

Hutchinson's conception of the kind of paper the *BOP*
should be was a far cry from that envisaged by the General
Committee of the RTS. They repeatedly rejected his
prototypes as being too secular and containing too little
moralising.[17] Believing it to be their duty to counteract the
pernicious penny-dreadfuls and other kinds of popular paper
freely available to young readers, the Committee wanted a
vigorously Christian weekly paper, sufficiently entertaining to
keep readers reading, but certainly not privileging
entertainment (by which they meant fiction of the adventure/
fantasy variety) over religiosity. Not surprisingly, they were
unable to sell their idea to any independent publisher. Having
decided that they must therefore bear the loss themselves, the
Committee asked G. A. Hutchinson, who had considerable
journalistic experience on religious and philanthropic
publications, to prepare the first number. Hutchinson was soon
at odds with his employers on the way to achieve their shared
objective of producing a salubrious Christian paper which
would effectively counteract the established low brand of
sensational publication.

Hutchinson felt strongly that a paper which essentially
consisted of evangelical tracts would fail to attract and cultivate
a young audience. The Committee responded to Hutchinson's
intransigence by placing Dr James Macaulay, the Society's
general secretary, over his head, and were no doubt chagrined
when Macaulay supported Hutchinson's views. Both men
recognised the great potential of fiction to capture the
imagination of young readers, and were convinced that the best
way to combat the 'bloods' and similar papers was with a
publication which offered equally exciting stories but which
nevertheless scorned the sordid subjects and sensational style of
its rivals. It was always around the subject of fiction that
debates over content raged. Hutchinson and Macaulay at last
obtained the reluctant permission of the General Committee to
produce the first few issues according to Hutchinson's design.
The official plan was to attract readers with early numbers

containing a high fiction/entertainment content, and then, on the principle of the thin end of the wedge, to increase the straightforwardly didactic Christian content. Fiction was never superseded, however, although Hutchinson continued to have to defend his policy both to the Committee and to other influential establishment figures.

The success of Hutchinson's formula was as immediate as it was unexpected. Within three months the circulation reached roughly 200,000, which Hutchinson believed gave them a readership of 600,000.[18] Deliberately priced at only a penny, it could be afforded by the same readers who purchased the penny-dreadfuls. Moreover, the *BOP* provided excellent value for money, being well designed, lavishly illustrated, printed on good-quality paper and frequently including colour pull-outs. It obviously succeeded in satisfying its young readers, for the year after its inception, the *BOP* was responsible for a considerable increase in the RTS receipts. Money at the time was badly needed to support overseas missionary work, so the paper which had been expected to be a loss maker began to finance the Society's more orthodox work. This fact undoubtedly strengthened Hutchinson's hand in sustaining the level of fiction in the paper. It probably also resulted in the launching of the even more successful sister publication, the *Girl's Own Paper*, in the following year.

Hutchinson and Reed's pronouncement about the aims of the *BOP* provides some interesting insights into the ambitions they had for the paper and the way they set about achieving them. The pair are not simply distancing themselves from the low papers on moral and ethical grounds, but are insisting upon the *quality* of their publication. Their emphasis on esteemed writers and experts is a clear indication of the line Hutchinson was taking. This emphasis was carried over into the pages of the paper, where no contributor was without some kind of recommendation. All are identified as experts in their fields, either through titles and awards, or as 'author of', or both, as in the case of the Reverend J. G. Wood, MA, FLS, 'author of *Illustrated Natural History*, etc.', whose practical natural history series frequently appeared in the *BOP*.

The controversial fiction content of the *BOP* (much of it written by established writers such as W. H. G. Kingston and R. M. Ballantyne) was the most popular and powerful aspect of the magazine. It was primarily through the fiction pages that Hutchinson saw the possibilities of establishing the reputation of the *BOP*. Hutchinson wanted his paper to crown the world of juvenile periodicals – to be the touchstone for quality reading matter.[19] To achieve this position he had to enlist the support of adults – in particular parents and educators.

For the most part the *BOP* seems to have succeeded in winning for its fiction, as well as for its more obviously practical and Christian features, the approval of its two audiences, as the following extracts from the correspondence columns of 17 September 1881 show.

'OUR SERIAL STORIES,' . . . . One writer, who takes forty-three copies of the BOY'S OWN PAPER for his Sunday-school, further shows that he has the 'success of the paper wholly at heart', by sending us something for our Note Book. Another correspondent writes from a Birkenhead school, in which 'upwards of 200 boys take the paper'. The head of a Dartford grammar-school writes: 'As a constant reader of the *Christian* as well as of the BOY'S OWN PAPER, I am so far qualified to give an opinion on both. I certainly would not place the former indiscriminately in the hands of my pupils . . . but the latter must change before I hesitate to permit its freest circulation, or cease to delight in its proving so great an attraction for boys.'
WORDS OF CHEER – The head of St. Joseph's School, Upper Norwood writes: 'I have been an admirer of the BOY'S OWN PAPER from the commencement, and must congratulate you heartily on its well-deserved success. The gentlemanly and healthy tone observable in all its pages is just what we require to counteract the influence of the pernicious trash with which the market is flooded. I have introduced it into the higher standards of the school as an occasional "reader", and I find that it answers well, and affords a pleasant variety in our reading lessons. I have also brought it under the notice of many of my professional brethren, and they have also found it useful.'

Here we have the ultimate commendation – used as a reader in the higher standards! Once in school, the status of the *BOP* was incontestable. In Board of Education schools it also succeeded in reaching an audience for whom the lessons in and mythology surrounding notions of appropriately masculine and gentlemanly behaviour would not be a preparation for life in boarding schools or in the outposts of empire, but a means of encouraging acceptance of the codes by which society at home was governed. The *BOP* had clearly distanced itself from the low-status comics, and found a favourable reception in the ideological institution primarily involved with young people.

Having succeeded in enlisting the support of adults and institutions on the grounds of content, Hutchinson continued his quest to secure high literary status for the paper. This meant that the fiction he included needed to incorporate what Shavit, in *The Poetics of Children's Literature* (1986), terms 'dual readership'. A narrative characterised by dual readership has to appeal simultaneously to readers of at least two different levels. That this was true of the *BOP* can easily be demonstrated, for the paper appealed to the different groups which comprised its audience in some obvious ways. One example is provided by the advertisements which appeared on the wrapper of the monthly part of the magazine. The *BOP* readership was *known* to consist of juvenile readers of both sexes, and of men. However, the advertisements suggest that mothers too scrutinised their sons' reading matter, for these included announcements about fabrics, furniture and prams as well as stamp albums, books, and bicycles.[20] Advertisements were one way of appealing separately to the different groups of readers. This kind of separation was also achieved through such things as competitions, which involved setting an upper age limit for the intended reader of the paper. After some fluctuation, this was agreed to be nineteen. While in one sense purely arbitrary, this decision had the effect of defining the official reader/ addressee of the *Boy's Own Paper* as a male under twenty years of age, thereby effectively splitting the readerships at a convenient numerical point.

The adult readers of the *BOP* responded to the paper in quite a different way from the boys to whom it was primarily addressed. Many saw themselves as watchdogs, scrutinising each number to be sure that all of the information, ideas and ideals conveyed were of the right sort. Teachers, clergymen and parents regularly engaged in pedantic correspondence with the editors over mistakes in spelling, grammar, syntax, Latin, theology and fact. It was not uncommon for the editors to receive letters correcting some slip years after it had occurred.[21]

The constant looking over the shoulder to make sure that its opinions were accurate and of the officially approved variety, which characterise much of the dual address in the pages of the *BOP*, is useful for understanding how the magazine functioned as a vehicle for the transmission of ideology and attitudes to sexual difference. Through its pages, and particularly through its serialised fiction, the *BOP* showed boys of what the prevailing construction of masculinity consisted. Dual readership implies a superior position from which the narrative is understood by the author and the experienced reader. This superior position encompasses an understanding of what are accepted as 'natural' and therefore right, values and modes of behaviour. The adult reader can adopt this position only in works which reflect his/her understanding of the world. Therefore, parents who wanted their sons to have something manly to read welcomed works which reinforced the qualities of mind and character associated with Victorian constructions of masculinity – the 'natural' goal for all boys.

In the *BOP*, such appropriate interests were demonstrably catered for. From its masthead, which shows an outdoor background against which are set cricket equipment, a football, a fishing rod, a gun dog and some rabbits – all elements of the active life advocated by Henty and Reed – through its practical, sporting, scientific and religious features, it never deviated from its task of appealing to and moulding the taste of the nation's youth.

A typical volume of the *BOP* contained a mixture of practical/instructional features and fiction. The practical pages were a characteristically late-Victorian mixture of facts, curiosities and do-it-yourself activities. These were supplemented by reports of famous battles and great figures from history. Such figures regularly appeared in the *BOP* and were unashamedly offered as models for the readers in series such as 'Boys Who Have Risen', and 'Youthful Honours Bravely Won'.

Perhaps the most revealing of all the non-fiction features in the *BOP* was its correspondence section. The numbers of questions answered testified to the use readers made of the service. However, curiously few of the replies deal with personal problems. In his feature on 'Camp Life For Boys' (3 September 1892), Dr Gordon Stables (who supplied medical advice as well as articles and stories) remarks that the editor received 'constant enquiries about how to grow tall, and about measurements of chest, calves, etc., and how to reduce fat'. These constant enquiries are given short shrift in the correspondence columns. Questions consist almost entirely of requests for information. It can only be conjectured how far this was deliberate policy. Where a scientific answer to a personal problem could be supplied, it was given, as in the reply to the youth who suffered from a tendency to blush.

> It so happens that the well-known English medical journal, the 'Lancet', has just been treating this very subject. . . . Blushing . . . is occasioned by sudden dilation of the small bloodvessels, which form a fine network beneath the skin. . . . The change effected in the size of the vessels is brought about by an instantaneous action of the nervous system. This action may be induced by a thought, or, unconsciously, by the operation of impressions producing the phenomenon habitually. In a word, blushing may become a habit, and is then beyond the control of the will, except in so far as the will can generally, if not always, conquer any habit.

The reader is encouraged to counter blushing with blanching, a response brought about by anger. This reply is interesting for the way in which it endeavours to transform a feeling regarded as effeminate (humiliation) and its tell-tale response (the blush) through the distancing achieved by treating the problem scientifically and reprocessing it through the masculine response of anger/aggression and mastery.

Fiction

Fiction was the mainstay of the *BOP*. It accounted for nearly 60 per cent of every issue, with at least two serials running consecutively and frequently short stories as well. According to Salmon, the *BOP*'s popularity was largely due to its adventure stories.[22] The prominence given to the fiction pages is indicative of the role they played in the paper's success. The front page always featured one of the serialised stories, including a large illustration. The first eight or nine pages were from the outset devoted to the stories of adventure or school life which characterised the fiction Hutchinson selected for the *BOP*. It is easy to see why adult readers approved of the fiction in the *BOP*. Just as Henty managed to impart a great deal of military and historical information in his books for boys, so the *BOP* contributors invariably managed to lace their works with some combination of instruction, information, moral guidance and/or a salutory message. If the stories were not always as didactic or improving as those by Reed, Hutchinson saw to it that they invariably had a high moral tone and showed behaviour appropriate to a Christian gentleman in whose hands lay the future of the Empire. But Hutchinson wanted more than approval. He wanted adult readers to respect and enjoy *BOP* fiction. To this end he brought in writers such as Jules Verne and Arthur Conan Doyle, both of whom had established themselves with adult audiences.

When one looks at the work of these writers published in the *BOP*, however, it soon becomes clear that the high status awarded to *BOP* fiction is not based on strictly literary qualities. It derives rather from a combination of acceptable morality, instruction, unimpeachable models, extensive vocabulary and the ability to tell a good story. A good example is provided by Jules Verne's *The Cryptogram; or 800 leagues of the Amazon*, which was serialised in the 1882 volume.

The story opens with a rather sophisticated critique of the westernisation of South America, but soon degenerates into a sensational adventure. It contains some instructive passages, including a number which offer lessons on the principles of physics, but it is really about murder, theft, disguise, discovery, and vindication for the hero. *The Cryptogram* is typical of *BOP* fiction: instructive, wholesome and entertaining, but not particularly good literature. There is no exploration of character, few noticeably well-written passages, little reflection on the nature of individuals and relationships, or the writing process. The appeal to adults is primarily through content – what the stories are about – rather than style – how they are told. The works achieve high status within the juvenile canon on these grounds and because they offer reassurance, not for their merit as literature. In fact, stories such as *The Cryptogram* are interesting as examples of the determination, characteristic of the authors of boys' fiction, to avoid becoming enmeshed in language. Language is used as a tool to explain, name, confirm and control situations and events. The code in Verne's story is cracked through industry, perseverence and the application of a systematic method. In this and the other *BOP* fiction, the reader is placed in the text in a position of knowledge, control and action. Confidence in self, country and the systems which bind the two is fostered. The young reader who is trying out constellations of words with which to name and place himself/herself in the world, will find in these stories a lexicon that has been loaded to give readers a flattering self-image. Just as a customer in a clothing store may be flattered by carefully chosen lights and mirrors, so male readers of this period were urged to believe that whatever their size, shape or intellectual ability, they could take for granted their status as men in a patriarchal society.

Thus, by choosing fiction which is never enigmatic, moves irresistibly towards closure, minimises the roles of reader/writer, looks outward rather than into the subject and attempts to instill confidence, the *BOP* joined in the movement in boys' fiction that was concerned with countering the notion that the current generation lacked 'the grit of its forefathers' by teaching boys what it meant to be truly male in late-Victorian and Edwardian England.[23]

Plate 1 This illustration from Hesba Stretton's story of London slum life (*Little Meg's Children*, 1868) shows the ten-year-old heroine nursing her dying baby sister. One of the most popular of the evangelical books for children, Stretton's work combines graphic descriptions of the conditions of the poor with a sentimental portrayal of the redemptive powers of childhood innocence. This image of childhood is in marked contrast to earlier, more Calvinistic works such as Mrs Sherwood's *The Fairchild Family* (1818) which were written to instruct sinful children in the need to turn to God.

Plates 2 and 3 (opposite) from Evelyn Everett-Green's *A Wilful Maid* clearly show the drive to reform those erring 'girls of the period'. From the fiercely independent and fashionable girl of the novel's opening, Lady Angela Goldhawk becomes a tearful and repentant young woman. At the book's conclusion she is happily married and, as her name had always foretold, soon to be the angel of her own household.

"SHE LAID HER HAND UPON THE BOWED HEAD."

Plate 4 'You are a wise maid to come to me to plead a wife's cause on behalf of an absent husband,' Queen Mary tells Lady Maud Melville. The three women in the picture, who are about to sort out the problems and misunderstandings made by bigoted and corrupt men, represent the myth of feminine power which provides self-esteem but depends on their not attempting to challenge the existing social order.

"'OH, HOW OBSTINATE SOME PEOPLE ARE !' REPLIED MAGGIE,
WEARILY."

Plate 5 This illustration from L. T. Meade's *A Sweet Girl Graduate* shows the brilliant Miss Maggie Oliphant adopting a suitably demure pose beside Senior Wrangler Geoffrey Hammond. Not surprisingly, the two are married by the end of the novel, and Maggie (who received a First Class degree) leaves academia behind for a more fulfilling career as wife and mother.

THE BROKEN CONTRACT

Plate 6 'The Broken Contract' appeared in 'Snow-drops', the extra Christmas issue for 1885. The theme of the overworked seamstress is familiar in Victorian painting; here the paper's concern for such young women is made more poignant by the arrival of the two girls (typical *GOP* readers?) for whom the dresses were being made.

Plate 7 The April 1882 number of the *GOP* featured the North London Collegiate School for Girls. The illustration shows one of Miss Buss's 'gymnasium teas'. The contrast between the girls' dainty and restrained attitudes and the activities in which they are purportedly engaging seems to epitomise the contradictory nature of late-Victorian attitudes about what constituted a nice young lady.

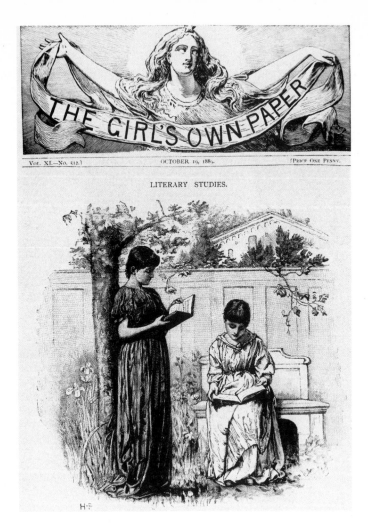

Plate 8 Front cover, *GOP*, 19 October 1889.

"SHE WOULD SIT AT MY FEET NIGHT AFTER NIGHT AND READ FROM THE BOOK ON MY LAP."

Plate 9 From the *GOP*, 10 May 1890.

Plate 10 This featured illustration accompanied a one-column story about obedience and piety. The picture shows one of the dominant images of femininity of this period – the invalid mother looking into the distance (probably indicating approaching death).

Plate 11 The new, more manly, embrace is typified in this illustration to R. M. Ballantyne's *Twice Bought* which was serialized in the *Boy's Own Annual* of 1883. Note the familiar mast-head with its many attributes illustrating typical male pursuits.

The Boy's Own
Model Steam Fire Engine
and how to make it. — by H.F.H.

There

Fire Engine of 1570

HFH

PART I.

Plate 12 The *BOP* regularly ran 'how-to-make-it' features such as this introduction to making a very complicated model steam engine which appeared in the 1889 annual.

"Coming events cast their shadows before."

Plate 13 Reproduced from the *Boy's Own Annual* of 1882.

DEATH RATHER THAN DISHONOUR.

Plate 14 This illustration, commissioned by the *BOP* and featured in the 29 December 1888 number, shows the paper's constant concern with promoting upright, courageous, Christian gentlemen. The nautical motif is equally characteristic.

"'SO, SIR, A SECOND TIME CAUGHT IN GROSS DECEIT!'"

Plate 15 This scene from Farrar's *Eric, or Little by Little* (1858) shows the wretched Eric at an early moment in his descent to depravity.

Plate 16 A typical selection of L. T. Meade's girls' stories. The rebellious heroines of the titles are inevitably tamed as their stories unfold.

Chapter 5

A literature of their own? Or what girls read

A Leal Light Heart by Annette Lyster . . . is a lively story in which the heroine is made to overcome many difficulties by her loyal nature and cheerful disposition. It ought to be a great favourite with girls.

The White Chapel by Esme Stuart ought to be a great favourite with girls; from the clever, interesting narrative there rises quite naturally the needful lesson of being considerate and thoughtful for others.

(from the SPCK catalogue for 1881)

'Thrown back on books, books, and again books.'

(from *The Diaries of Beatrice Webb*, November 1882)

The emergence of separate literatures for boys and girls in late-Victorian and Edwardian England is usually explained as one more example of the contemporary tendency to divide the sexes into separate spheres along the lines Ruskin describes in *Sesame and Lilies*. Thus boys were to be introduced to worldly matters in their fiction, whilst in the books they read, girls were to be protected from any shadow which might taint their purity. According to this theory, boys were basically free to read what they liked, while surrounding girls' reading there was a substantial, public debate in which advice, cautions and strictures were freely expressed.[1]

The accuracy of this explanation must be questioned, for it does not tally with the evidence. I have argued that far from having great freedom in their literary choice, boys were subjected to considerable pressure to restrict their reading of fiction. They were to confine themselves to books conveying approved images of masculinity, manly attitudes and forms of address and information which would promote material success. As will become apparent, girls' reading at end of the century equally defies conventional understanding. There is a noteworthy contradiction between what girls actually read, the prohibitive rhetoric which laid down what they ought and ought not be reading, and what in fact it was tacitly accepted that girls read. The reason for this discrepancy seems to lie in the shaping of girls' reading tastes, especially in school and in the literature written specifically for them. It seems likely that those areas of approved reading worked together to ensure that what was read was of less importance than *how it was understood.*

There *was* anxiety about girls' reading. It arose from what Charlotte M. Yonge identified as their 'indiscriminate appetite for fiction', which meant that girls were likely to read fiction intended for a variety of different and frequently inappropriate audiences.[2] This was perceived as problematic, for girls were considered to be highly suggestible. As it was socially imperative that their innocence be preserved if their marriage prospects were not be be impaired, it was deemed necessary to ensure that they did not come into contact with corrupting or dubious material in the books they read. For much of the century reading matter for girls was vetted by parents, guardians, educationists, critics and even publishers, and suitable works listed and put before them.[3] The problem was that most of the books which made up the acceptable canon of girls' literature at mid-century were fairly tedious and certainly tame tales of domestic life. Frequently these were no more than handbooks for good behaviour loosely held together by an unexciting story. As a consequence, girls infinitely preferred to read novels, or the books of adventure directed at their brothers. The contents of such works, however, were deemed to be totally unsuited for consumption by young ladies. Novels, intended for a more mature audience, were likely to contain references, attitudes and incidents with which they should not be familiar. This was also true of the books written for their male peers, for while the Victorians believed that a woman became unwomanly with knowledge of the world, they also held that 'a man could not truly be a man unless he had seen stripped bare the tree of the fruit of knowledge of good and evil.'[4] The boys' books accordingly contained examples of lying, cheating, stealing and other vices from which girls were to be protected.

But as girls continued to demand more exciting books and to risk charges of unladylike behaviour by secretly imbibing the contents of their brothers' libraries, it became evident that there was a need (and a market) for a literature which could satisfy their appetite for entertainment without the accompanying danger of corruption.

One way of doing this was to incorporate appropriate models for girls into suitable boys' adventure stories. This endeavour contributed significantly to the development of that branch of juvenile publishing directed jointly at boys and girls, for it gave rise to those depictions of late-Victorian and Edwardian bourgeois family life which have become the 'classics' of children's literature. Such books (typified in the works of Mrs Ewing, Frances Hodgson-Burnett, and E. Nesbit) replace the ethos of confidence, mastery and independence based on masculine superiority with one based on class. In them sex roles are unambiguous, and accordingly the adventures have been domesticated (so as to rule out potentially compromising situations for the female characters and readers): the emphasis is on celebrating family life rather than on conquering foreign lands and exotic peoples. Such books are primarily concerned with instructing readers in acceptable social and moral behaviour; what is important is the lessons the fictional children learn about their responsibilities for others.

Significantly, both boys' fiction and the domestic adventure studiously ignore changes and challenges to established notions of femininity and the role of women. In boys' books, women are notable by their absence. Most adventures begin with a departure from home and mother (if she is alive), and from that moment female characters are conscientiously excluded. There are occasional cameo appearances in the form of wives of headmasters, generals, or other men-in-charge, and sometimes there are even token sweethearts whom the returning hero marries in the last paragraph, but essentially there are no female characters in books for boys. The attitude to women such books convey is entirely consistent with the domestic ideal; all good women stay at home, tend to domestic affairs and have babies.

By contrast, those books which depict middle-class family life provide quite a lot of information about female roles, though again they refuse to acknowledge any challenge to the feminine ideal. In *The Madwoman in the Attic* (1979), Gilbert and Gubar call attention to the fact that in life and in the literature of the last century there appear to have been a startling number of invalid women. They suggest that these enfeebled females can be regarded as metaphorically rich, for the many late-Victorian and Edwardian women who became paralysed physically, intellectually and/or emotionally comprise an eloquent testimony to the power of the contradictory notions of womanhood which surrounded the contemporary construction of femininity. These divided women into two exclusive categories: the pure, passive and passionless angel in the house, and her counterpart, the whore or madwoman. These rigid categories (the boundary between which can be likened to a mirrored maze – fragile, distorting and shifting) were elaborated and spread so effectively that they seemed literally to undermine women. Indeed, Gilbert and Gubar suggest that the brand of patriarchy typical of late nineteenth- and early twentieth-century England actually promoted female sickness as a goal, surrounding women with 'images of disease, traditions of disease and invitations both to disease and to dis-ease'.[5]

It is certainly true that in those juvenile books concerned with family life there is a succession of invalid women who are held up as models of the feminine ideal; they tend to be white-faced, frail and prone to headaches. Their infrequent appearances in the narratives typically find them prostrated on their day-beds whilst frequent applications of *eau-de-Cologne* are applied to their aching temples by ministering daughters. These women are classic idols to the nineteenth-century cult of domesticity. Beautiful, dependent and imbued with the property of causing those around them to wish to be good, when, as invariably happens, these angelic ladies find themselves temporarily deprived of husbands and incomes, they contrive to earn a living in a way which accentuates their intrinsic adherence to established social norms. This is usually through writing (of an appropriate kind – 'little pieces' and children's stories), needlework or painting. Their brave little successes are applauded, but I have yet to come across a single such mother in juvenile fiction who was able to provide sufficient money for her family's needs or who in any way became a business success or even enjoyed the break from ordinary domestic life. To do so would have transgressed the bounds of femininity and unfitted her for the drawing-room, to which she is ultimately destined to return.

A possible exception to this pattern is found in the countless 'vinegar aunts' whose short tempers tend to obscure considerable domestic skills, and to belie warm hearts. The implication is generally that shrewish tempers are a consequence of thwarted fulfilment. Unable to find husbands for themselves, these 'odd women' become dependent on relations and have to justify their presence by energetic demonstrations of domestic utility. Their managerial skills may equally suggest frustration in their professional lives. It is not insignificant that such characters are never mothers. This appears to be a further example of splitting positive and negative aspects of important figures identified by Bettelheim in relation to the fairy tale.[6]

An equally frequent device in children's fiction of this period was to have the mother, whose death highlights her feminine virtues, become, almost literally, an angel. A household without a mother calls attention to her skills and abilities by running idiosyncratically. Alive or dead, mothers in these books are always martyrs to the domestic ideal. They are passive, dependent, supportive and regulated. These stories refuse to grapple with the challenges to the imaging of women which were then taking place and which *were* being reflected in literature for adults. The 'New Woman' and her young counterpart, 'the girl of the period', with their short hair, loose habits and challenging behaviour, do not intrude into the golden afternoons of these stories. The little girls who go on adventures with their brothers and cousins are never in any danger of straying from the domestic ideal.

Neither the boys' story nor the bourgeois fantasy was very much concerned specifically with being attractive to or suitable for girls. They had no need to be, for a more enduring and effective solution to the problem caused by what girls were reading was achieved by creating a new and exciting literature especially for girls in which nothing morally compromising ever took place and in which there was no challenge to accepted notions about the feminine ideal. The need for such a literature was intensified as adult fiction (some of which girls were likely to have sampled) began to be increasingly concerned with reflecting contemporary attempts to redefine the female role. This was frequently done by depicting and exploring the motivation behind the 'New Woman'.

Early feminists and their allies were making increasingly vociferous attacks on the cult of domesticity, with its ethos of self-sacrifice and service on the part of women and its tendency to regard women relationally rather than as individuals. The inclusion of rebellious or unconventional women in novels simultaneously reported and helped to bring about change in the female role.[7] This in turn facilitated further change, so that by the end of the century, the central female characters in many novels were totally at odds with the social construction of femininity which had prevailed for decades. Around such pioneer heroines as Dorothea Brooke, Rhoda Nunn and Herminia Barton, the novel incorporated a discourse which explored the need for female emancipation, women's right to self-determination, the recognition and acceptance of female sexuality and the legitimate right of women to act independently. The gradual change in the depiction of heroines in adult fiction drew on actual incidents and trends and helped to accustom the reading public to the New Women. The relationship between fictional characters and their flesh-and-blood counterparts can therefore be described as both symbiotic and productive.

If true of adult fiction, this relationship must also pertain in fiction for girls. It is therefore important to look at representations of women in the new-style fiction for girls to see what kind of cross-fertilisation is taking place: to what kind of roles, expectations, and norms its young readers were becoming accustomed.

The imaging of women in nineteenth-century fiction for girls

At first glance, the succession of young rebels and madcaps who are the central characters in many of the new girls' stories appear to be youthful versions of the rebellious heroines in adult fiction. The girl rebel was characterised as outspoken, intelligent, a marvellous story-teller and instigator of outrageous schemes. She often behaved wildly, was wilful and revelled in unconventional behaviour. In spite of these superficial features, which seem to be embracing a new image of womanhood and a revised notion of femininity, these 'naughty' girls exist as part of a convention which is as reactionary as its adult counterpart was radical. In girls' fiction, the tenacity of the traditional representation of acceptable womanhood is clear: the old ideal is perpetuated, not eradicated. Indeed, one of the most interesting features of this new literature is the way it takes details from contemporary debate about the behaviour associated with the new imaging of women, and contrasts them with the internal values identified with old notions of femininity. The result is an essentially conservative attack on the 'girl of the period'.

The discrepancy between the presentation of attractively wayward girls who, their authors initially suggest, are representative of new values, and the traditional values they actually confirm is the result of a number of factors. One of these is the general conservatism characteristic of children's literature which extends from subject matter to a concern with preserving conventional narrative strategies. Children's literature resists change at all levels.[8]

It is also important to note that this fiction specifically written for girls evolved roughly forty years after challenges to conventional representations of femininity were introduced into the adult novel.[9] Studies of societies which have undergone similar pressures to change the status of women have shown that after even the most profound social upheavals there has invariably been a return to full patriarchy.[10] In accordance with this pattern, a conservative backlash towards the end of the nineteenth century could be explained as the consequence of a vigorous campaign and some successes in changing the status of women.

An alternative but related explanation is that the anti-progressive discourse in these texts is the result of unease on the part of those who controlled institutions such as publishing houses, schools and churches. It follows that the more the old domestic ideal was being challenged in practice, the more it was insisted upon in representations, and particularly those directed at the next generation of women.

Another factor which may help to explain the contradictory nature of these old-fashioned, new-fashioned girls can perhaps be laid at the door of the pioneers of women's education. Prominent figures such as Frances Mary Buss and her staff at the North London Collegiate School, and the founder of Westfield College, Constance Maynard, found themselves espousing a doctrine which was innately contradictory. While they advocated education, liberation and careers on the one hand, each was firmly committed to conventional images and aspirations of Victorian femininity. Buss, in fact, regularly read her girls passages from Coventry Patmore's *The Angel in the House*, suggesting it was the ultimate goal to which they should aspire.[11] Though convinced that education was essential for young women, they saw its first objective as being the improvement of motherhood. Only those who failed to achieve the status of wife and mother were encouraged to look for careers and independence.

The common ground between each of these factors is that old-style Victorian images of femininity continued to be handed down to young girls and that a primary vehicle for transmitting these values was the new fiction for girls. The final chapter looks in detail at the way in which popular authors inscribed this definition of femininity as right and natural, using language, structure and content to encourage readers to position themselves in a way which helped to reconcile changes in life-style and opportunities with the traditional definition of femininity. First it is important to consider the implications of this drive on girls' reading.

Girls' reading habits

Study of girls' fiction at the time in which it was becoming a distinct category within juvenile publishing reveals an interesting, frequently contradictory progression. First, girls were identified as omnivorous readers. This resulted in anxiety about the possible effects of reading on their adherence to established notions of femininity, which in turn led to the creation of a special literature for girls. This special literature was widely read by girls *in addition* to their other reading: it was not a replacement for other kinds of fiction. What is significant is that as girls' fiction became an established part of most girls' early reading experience, anxiety about what else was read seems to have diminished. More interestingly still, in spite of their having a mighty body of fiction written specifically to appeal to them and to school them in desirable manners and mores, girls were seldom subjected to the kinds of pressures put on boys that limited and prescribed their reading matter and habits, nor were these pressures, when they were applied, so pronounced or effective. Thus while the anxiety about keeping girls pure had not lessened, there was nevertheless an increased acceptance of their reading a wide selection of fiction. Why should this be?

It seems likely that a key to this tolerance can be located in the success of the new girls' fiction in creating a reader who could be relied upon to read – and probably to select – safely. By drawing readers into ideological and discursive positions which encouraged them to accept as right and natural the existing social structure, with its profoundly inconsistent, frequently perverse and prohibitive attitudes towards women, these books together became a lens through which all other fictions were likely to be perceived and filtered. Meaning is released as part of the reading process – to a large extent the reader reads the book s/he creates from the words on the page. Therefore, the habitual reading position acquired through regular reading of girls' fiction would inevitably affect other reading. Furthermore, because such works give the impression of resolving conflict and offer fantasy-alternatives to difficult or uncongenial realities, they may set up a kind of dependency in the reader who wishes to regain the pleasurable sensation of harmony, resolution and emotional gratification they offer.[12] The reading of girls' fiction can therefore be seen as a slip road into women's reading of popular fiction, which in the nineteenth century tended to be comprised of the kind of three-volume novel from Mudie's which George Eliot titled the 'mind-and-millinery species',[13] and today of the romance fiction typified by the Mills and Boon series.

The new girls' fiction, then, cultivated a taste for fiction generally, and low-status romance and sensation novels in particular. It also gave birth to a reader who had the potential and the desire to recreate whatever she read into something related to the pleasurable reading with which she was most familiar. The impetus for this transformation was not generated solely at the level of plot. It depended largely on a combination of textual features, many of which are also associated with popular fiction; a fact which must have contributed to girls' fiction being denied literary merit.

The seductive powers of popular fiction for women, and its tendency to reconcile women to patriarchy, have recently given rise to a number of interesting studies which examine women's reading habits in the twentieth century.[14] The features identified in women's fiction of our own time, especially that of maintaining the status quo in gender relations, were recognised a century ago and resisted by at least some of the less conventional women of the time. Florence Nightingale railed against the three-volume novel in *Cassandra* (1852–59), as did George Eliot in 'Silly novels by lady novelists' (1856). Beatrice (Potter) Webb's journals are full of resolutions to discipline herself away from reading romantic and other fiction thought suitable for young ladies and to establish a reading programme modelled on male education.

The interesting thing about Webb's comments (which are typical of many Victorian and Edwardian women who wished to cultivate their intellectual powers) is the way she feels she must be weaned away from 'suitable' literature – to smash the lens and see, as she thinks it, properly. This attitude is consistent with the classification of girls' fiction as meretric-ious: a substratum within juvenile publishing. It also identifies the reading of girls' fiction with failure to gain parity with men, as lacking the privileged masculine discourse which charac-terises accredited literature and as intellectually detrimental.

The status of fiction for girls

The tendency to regard all books for girls as lacking literary merit needs to be questioned as the real *raison d'être* behind their poor standing. Evidence that books for girls were quickly designated as a separate, low-status area of juvenile publishing abounds, but this phenomenon is not as straightforward as it might appear. Momentarily leaving aside the problems raised by the eclectic nature of girls' reading, there remain a number of incongruities in this classification. Many of these can be explained by referring back to the attitudes towards the reading of fiction discussed in the preceding chapters. While boys were warned against reading fiction, ostensibly on the grounds that it wasted time, encouraged inappropriate fantasies and ruined their chances of a successful life (perhaps because it was in some sense regarded as unmanning them), girls were positively encouraged to read appropriate fiction, both at home and at school.[15] Furthermore, carefully regulated reading was desir-able for middle-class girls as it relieved boredom, was a harmless occupation and one which girls looked nice doing – they were frequently painted reading.[16] It could also be argued that reading fiction was perceived as a desirable activity for girls because it steered them into an open-ended channel in which they could wallow in fantasy and imaginary resolutions to social and sexual problems (resolutions which, because not genuine, needed constantly to be repeated) and generally gave them an activity and a language which impeded social success based on individuality, activity and self-confidence.

Reading fiction was not perceived as an intellectual activity *per se*. When girls did take an interest in novels of recognised merit, this interest was not always encouraged or taken seriously. For instance, in Salmon's *Juvenile Literature as it is*, the responses to a survey conducted in schools are presented to the reader with a caveat to suspect the girls' answers. This is because among their ten favourite authors the girls numbered Dickens (1), Scott (2), Kingsley (3), Shakespeare (5), Eliot (8) and Lord Lytton (9). Salmon concludes that these authors were chosen, not because girls genuinely liked or had read their works, but because they were associated with or known from school and were therefore thought to be the right names to put forward. He also suggests that these names were well known and easily remembered while the names of those who wrote fiction regarded as more appropriate for girls were less easily recalled.

Salmon's desire to discount the girls' replies (and it is significant that he accepts the boys' unreservedly although their survey was carried out under the same conditions) is consistent with a widespread body of opinion which held that girls should be reading books which were suitable for their age and expectations. Charlotte M. Yonge encapsulated this attitude in *What Books to Lend and Give*. Of the tale for girls she writes:

> Those for whom they are written really do read and like them. There are so many hours in a girl's life when she must sit still, that a book is her natural resource, and reading becomes to her like breathing. The real difficulty is how to prevent the childish reading of story-books from becoming a preparation for unmitigated novel reading in after-life.
>
> (p. 454)

Salmon and Yonge concur that there is a need for girls' fiction which makes a bridge between the nursery and the drawing-room. While Yonge insists that the girls liked their fiction as it was (nevertheless noting that they also avidly read their brothers' book whenever possible), Salmon identifies an insufficiency in the genre if taken as an exclusive literary diet. He suggests that girls looked beyond their own literature because it was often too passive and 'goody-goody'. Both perceive girls' stories to be inferior to those written for boys or for a mixed audience.

In *The Poetics of Children's Literature*, Shavit argues convincingly that within the field of literature (the 'literary polysystem'), children's literature is consistently devalued. Also, that if a work of juvenile fiction appeals to adults as something they like to read (rather than something which is didactically suitable for young readers), this is either the result of its being 'ambivalent' (consisting of more than one level of writing and therefore directed at more than one kind of reader) or appealing to a more experienced reader on the basis of originality of form or subject. Children's literature is profoundly conservative, but occasionally original texts are generated (often these are works which have failed to gain acceptance as adult fiction – perhaps on the grounds of subject matter or the age or type of central characters). Such texts have regularly evaded strict classification. For instance, the prototypes of the adventure and school stories for boys are regarded as a class 'written for boys, but intended to be read by men'.[17] These books avoid the low literary status generally associated with children's fiction; they become the top grade of juvenile publishing and may escape into an honorary category of adult fiction.

Other books in the mainstream of children's fiction (where originality operates as well) have been up-graded in a similar way. Works such as *Alice in Wonderland* (1865), and Lear's *A Book of Nonsense* (1845) have always enjoyed success, largely on the basis of their popularity with adults.

Neither of these avenues into adult fiction (which designates a work as high in status within the juvenile canon) is open to girls' fiction. Thus it seems that status is based more on intended audience than readership.[18] Girls' fiction is, as far as it is possible to be, characterised by a unified, self-contained address, and this is not because it fails to capture a more sophisticated audience, but *refuses* to do so. The consequence is that the path to becoming accepted as high-status literature based on language and address is blocked by rejection of dual readership. The passport of originality is equally inaccessible since books designated as fiction for girls are invariably reworking existing themes and literary forms, even when these are relatively new to publishing as was the case with the girls' school story.

Because it failed to meet the usual requirements for acceptance as high-status juvenile literature, was written by women and read by girls, the new girls' fiction was assumed to lack literary merit. Its offerings were set aside as an uninteresting but useful mass of pulp. This became the starting point from which books for girls came to be seen as a sub-genre within the already devalued areas of juvenile publishing. The accuracy of this *de facto* dismissal of girls' fiction needs to be questioned, as does the motivation behind it.

Much of the popular fiction not intended for girls – especially that in comics and largely directed at boys – was associated with working-class culture.[19] It cultivated violence, vulgar humour and disrespect for adults, authorities and institutions. The language is simple and regularly includes usage condemned by educated, middle-class adults. The plots are unsubtle, generally sensational, often take place in exotic settings and have to do with personal problems which appeal to the emotions rather than the intellect. The stories are frequently amoral and reject didacticism in every form, generally ending with the physical humiliation of figures representing authority. At every level these works reject adults and adult values and particularly those associated with upper and middle-class adults.

In between this kind of popular fiction and those works accorded high status within the juvenile canon existed the large body of stereotypical and formulaic stories which tended to borrow themes, plots and characters from earlier successful works; notably school, adventure and mystery tales. They share with comics dependence on repetitive and formulaic plots, the use of officially discouraged language and the rejection of adults, both as active participants within the plot and as desired readers. Addressed exclusively to the child and not attempting to woo the adult through language, subject or pedagogic value, they exemplify the 'univalent' text.[20]

There were equivalents to the 'bloods' and thrillers written for boys which were directed at female readers. While the subject matter of these magazines might be regarded as feminised, being more concerned with love, jealousy and suicide rather than murder, mayhem and militancy, the evidence provided by style and structure suggests that they actually belong to the same working-class category as their male counterparts.[21] This is because the majority of early fiction for girls, while regarded as low in status on the grounds that it lacks literary quality and popular on the basis of numbers produced and size of readership, nevertheless fails to conform to many of the characteristics of other kinds of lowly regarded mass-marketed juvenile fiction. For instance, while these texts operate on a level which never seeks to address or involve a more sophisticated audience, they do not reject adults. Parents or parent-figures (headmistresses, clerics, relations, doctors and other advisers) often feature prominently, and far from the girl-heroine's having to effect change and resolution on her own, may be directly responsible for bringing it about through good counsel or actual intervention of one kind or another. The language used is similarly designed to reflect adult values. The vocabulary is often complex and varied, and lines are quoted from, or other references made to, respected literary texts. Both of these elements assume wide literary experience and a degree of reading skill. Where questionable usage (usually in the form of slang or regional dialect) occurs, it is almost invariably for the sake of creating an authentic atmosphere (for example, that of school) and has often disappeared by the end of the book (a sign of the heroine's growing maturity and acceptance of adult values). There is no deliberate, sustained, or in any sense approved demonstration of disrespect for adults of the same social class, no vulgar humour; there are no exotic settings, or physical triumphs. The working-class elements of popular juvenile fiction are eschewed. Thus the content of the new girls' fiction aligned it with the high-status, classic children's literary culture of late-Victorian and Edwardian England, whilst its repetitive nature, refusal to admit new models, acceptance of only the known and familiar and univalent discourse link it to the low-status, popular, juvenile fiction.[22]

The correspondence between popular fiction and the new

girls' fiction breaks down on two central and related points: the attitude towards adult authority conveyed and the kind of language used. This being the case, it is worth considering the nature of the univalent discourse which contributes to girls' fiction's being classified as popular/poor literature.

Adult authority is generally accepted and appreciated in these texts (which in part may have accounted for their commercial success since adults were largely responsible for purchasing and distributing girls' fiction although not inclined to read or value the works as literature). They only and in minor ways offend against linguistic orthodoxy. Thus, the single level of address in these books cannot be regarded as the same as examples from mainstream children's fiction which seek to flout authority and rebel against adult codes typified by 'correct' usage. The result of this rebellion is that, far from being truly univalent, much of the fiction which was most popular with young people (e.g. comics, magazines and thrillers) constantly employed and drew attention to other discourses in their insistence on being different. The single level (us against them) at which they purport to be communicating is actually refracted, and its elements shown to be made up of conflicting voices rising from the fragmentation, competition and cultural interactions which characterised England at the end of the last century. These competing discourses are celebrated in popular fiction and the antagonism between classes, races, ages and sexes which fills the pages of the penny-dreadfuls and novelettes, accounts for much of their humour and robustness.

The language characteristic of girls' fiction is markedly different. The difference can be best described by borrowing some of the terms and theories devised by M. M. Bakhtin to facilitate his discussion of the novel, for Bakhtin explores the relationship between external, essentially ideological pressures on language, which I have described as seminal to internal, psychic development and so central to the formation of sexual identity. Of particular interest is Bakhtin's conception of the novel as comprised of different kinds of language juxtaposed in a way which emphasises that they are in conflict. He makes a distinction between this kind of variform, interacting or 'heteroglossic' language, and that he terms 'monoglossic'. Bakhtin associates monoglossia with stable, pre-capitalist societies. Such societies he sees as demonstrating a tendency to work for a united dominant language which refuses to acknowledge any gap between language and reality. The dominant language may absorb elements from dialects, slang and jargon; it is not rigid or impervious to change. However, once isolated, rogue elements are integrated into the dominant language, they become part of the standard usage and lose their irregular status. This process is consistent with reflecting a unified vision of society. However, if the dominant language is forced to be omnivorous because of widespread challenges and claims, then it breaks down, fragments and becomes heteroglossic.

The reasons for the breakdown of unified language are many; among them Bakhtin cites the intense activity and cultural change brought about by such things as war, internal political and/or economic upheavals, interchange resulting from trade or exploration, and scientific or technological discoveries. All of these factors were at work in the second half of the nineteenth century.

Bakhtin associates monoglossia with stability, confidence and the 'classical body' (e.g. representations characterised by harmony, proportion, maturity, idealisation and an emphasis on things cerebral, pure and serious). Heteroglossia's characteristic articulation of transition and the question of established values Bakhtin connects with the 'grotesque body' of misrule, inversion, anti-intellectualism, carnality and the lower bodily functions.[23]

In Bakhtin's formulation, monoglossia is impossible after the Renaissance. The rise of the novel he gives as evidence that unified language can no longer exist. However, in many ways early girls' fiction can best be understood as adhering to monoglossic principles. While other popular forms of children's literature (and popular literature generally), with its delight in violence, vulgarity and the victimisation of those in authority, is clearly heteroglossic and concerned with aspects of the grotesque body, so girls' fiction is not.[24]

In spite of the fact that the new literature for girls originated in a period of intense social change and one in which the role of women was particularly volatile, it is characterised by language which attempts to deny change and the resulting linguistic divisions it engenders. The texts seek to gloss over the existence of other, problematic discourses and to create the impression that the language of fiction is a stable medium portraying an equally stable world. Some token elements of slang and jargon have been absorbed and the dialogue often includes fragments of dialects (and an apparently universal concern with rendering the childish lisp), yet through the pasteurising hand of the author, these become a homogenised product. In Bakhtin's terms, the texts are monoglossic and accordingly represented by the idealised classical body. This takes the form of concern with things spiritual, typified by idealisations, striving after maturity, a determination to represent the world as harmonious and a devoted seeking after and bowing before the altar of things intellectual. Thus the monoglossic language and accompanying classical body concerns and images in early girls' fiction make a linguistic structure which is fundamentally inconsistent, for it simultaneously encourages readers to respect and accept the validity of male-dominated, academic credos and discourses, while perceiving them as incompatible with the spirituality and purity of the feminine ideal.

The identification of monoglossia with a stable, confident society makes its presence in girls' fiction significant. At a time when there was considerable social turbulence, not least surrounding the role of women, traditionally regarded as the guardians and transmitters of culture, it seems likely that a literature specifically directed at the coming generation of women would seek to contain and minimise change. In the final years of the century attempts were, in fact, made to do this in a variety of media, because it was believed that reform should be gradual and organic.[25] But the authors and publishers of girls' fiction differ from others who made these attempts in that they tried not only to control the pace of change, but actually to reverse its progress. In this monoglossic language plays a crucial role: it allows topical inflections which appeal to young readers, facilitates the use of classic realism whereby the reader is drawn into the text to form an alliance with the implied author and excludes conflicting narrative modes or vocabularies. It also supports the institutional language of school and guides the reader into a position from which she perceives herself to be intellectually inferior and is encouraged to be passive and conformist. By using monoglassic language, these works were able to assimilate key words and phrases from the debates surrounding women. As soon as these expressions were incorporated in the dominant language, they lost their power to shock and challenge. Monoglossia thus provides a linguistic strategy which both mirrored and buttressed the structures and contents of the new fiction for girls in late-Victorian and Edwardian England. The widespread use of this pattern, with its combination of internal and external cues, is apparent in the stories which form the basis of the final chapter.

Chapter 6

Angel voices: Evelyn Everett-Green, L. T. Meade and the **Girl's Own Paper**

THE GIRL'S OWN PAPER

RULES.

I. No charge is made for answering questions.

II. All Correspondents to give initials or pseudonym.

III. The Editor reserves the right of declining to reply to any of the questions.

IV. No direct answers can be sent by the Editor through the post.

V. No more than two questions may be asked in one letter, which must be addressed to the Editor of THE GIRL'S OWN PAPER, *56, Paternoster Row, E.C.*

VI. No addresses of firms, tradesmen, or any other matter of the nature of an advertisement will be inserted.

A sermon is not to tell you what you are, but what you ought to be, and a novel should tell you not what you are to get, but what you'd like to get. . . . Real life is sometimes so painful.

(Lily Dale in Chapter 42 of *The Small House at Allington*, 1862–4, by Anthony Trollope)[1]

If late-Victorian and Edwardian girls' stories were considered reactionary and looked down upon, what of the women who wrote them (for most were written by women, though edited, published, and marketed by men)? Were they aware of the conservative and regressive nature of their writing? Did they adhere to the feminine ideal themselves? Or were they perhaps required to write what would be acceptable to editors, publishers, and adult purchasers, whilst inwardly rebellious? Is there any evidence of the kind of 'authentic female voice' which feminist criticism has identified in many adult novels by women before and during this period?[2]

It was possible to consider together the lives and works of two popular authors of books for boys and to make educated guesses as to the way in which they perceived themselves and their public roles. It was my intention to repeat this process for two similarly established writers for girls: Evelyn Everett-Green (1856–1932) and L. T. Meade (1879–1914). The pair seemed particularly interesting as, apart from Enid Blyton, they are the most prolific writers for children ever, and though they wrote many books for both sexes, have come to be primarily associated with girls' fiction. Their books, many of which were issued as rewards or prizes, are still widely available in second-hand book shops, but at a fraction of what would be paid for a Henty or Reed in similar condition. Although sometimes collected as attractive examples of nineteenth-century juvenile publishing, their books are rarely bought for their contents. The disparity between the value placed on the works of Everett-Green and Meade, and those of Henty and Reed is mirrored in the interest taken in their lives. Although Reed's biography was not written until 1960, his papers and much relating to him had been preserved and were available to Morrison when at last he settled down to his long-delayed project. Henty's life was fully recorded immediately after his death and care has subsequently been taken to collect and document Henty memorabilia. By contrast, it has proved all but impossible to locate material about the two women writers.

That the material was unavailable, despite the fact that both women made considerable impressions on generations of young readers and were 'bread and butter' writers for their publishers, is in itself interesting as an indicator of the value placed on their work. They were not unimportant in their day. Their books were regularly reviewed in serious journals and newspapers, including *The Times*. Meade, in particular, was conscious of and exercised her influence when she took on responsibility for *Atalanta*, a girls' literary magazine. *Atalanta* was concerned with showing that girls and young women had intellectual interests and sophisticated taste in literature. Its pages were filled primarily with quality fiction by established authors as well as information about and digested versions of 'classic' texts such as the works of Scott, Coleridge, Jane Austen, Carlyle and Dickens. There were scholarship pages which set essays to be sent in to the editorial panel; an *Atalanta* debating club, and fine art pages and competitions. Art and the professional advancement of women tended to fill the non-fiction pages. There were features on contemporary painters and a monthly page headed 'Employment for Girls'. Here readers received advice about training, fees, examinations and apprenticeships.

The assumption in the early numbers of *Atalanta* was that girls wished to have their taste in literature developed. Pages were densely printed with few illustrations and serialised novels were presented in much longer instalments than in other girls' papers. Shortly, however, the emphasis changed. It may have been that *Atalanta* was not financially secure; certainly the change in content seems to have been an attempt to appeal to a wider audience. Shorter romance stories began to be included by the time the end of the first volume had been reached; volume ten carried at least two major romantic serials. Other changes also occurred. Perhaps the most significant were in the attitudes to higher education and training for employment. The original professional page, 'Employment for Girls', was replaced by 'Occupations for Gentlewomen' which, instead of giving advice about careers as typists, civil servants, chromo lithographists, pharmacists and journalists, considered more traditionally ladylike ways of earning money. Among these were teaching, lacework, embroidery, painting and nursing.

Girls who went to college and who might have been considered the audience at which the magazine was primarily directed were not presented first and foremost as serious scholars. In 'Women Students at Oxford' (vol. 2), the emphasis is on the joys of tea, bicycling, and cocoa parties. These are the interests that Meade highlights in her schoolgirl fiction, but seem to be in marked contrast to her original plans for *Atalanta*. This raises questions about Meade's real interests and beliefs and about the work she produced; in particular, how far she was constrained by publishers and a fixed notion of what suited the girls' market.

Although concerned mostly with fiction, *Atalanta* attempted to show its readers (and the publishing world) that girls' fiction need not be considered as a separate category. Girls' fiction, it declared, was fiction read by girls and included that belonging to the high-status portions of the adult and boys' canon. By showing girls to be capable of reading and enjoying good literature, Meade, through *Atalanta*, was aligning herself with those educational reformers who rejected separate syllabuses for young men and women. Paradoxically, the way in which the magazine went about encouraging its readers to respond to literature may have had exactly the opposite effect. Rather than enabling girls to show themselves to be on an intellectual par with their male cohort, *Atalanta* encouraged them to follow the route laid out within the educational system where English language and composition had become the province of girls and Board of Education schools. Asked to respond to prose, poetry and plays, girls explored their emotions in neat, well-phrased essays, but failed to learn how to construct a critique of the society in which they lived and were controlled. Expert in fictional relationships and qualities, they were unfamiliar with the structural relations within their culture and pleasantly distracted from realising that this was so. The essays they produced sought to emulate male education (thereby assuming its values including attitudes towards women and social organisation) and to please authority.

In the discussion of L. T. Meade's stories which follows, it becomes evident that her books are consistently structured so as to underline traditional images of femininity and to undermine the attractions of changes to women's roles. However, she was clearly interested in showing that girls were intellectually capable, and through *Atalanta* seemed to try to appeal to and foster a new, more educated audience. This, together with the fact that she belonged to a feminist club, The Pioneers, suggests that her books may have been influenced by pragmatic considerations and publishers' advice.[3]

Evelyn Everett-Green

The daughter of an artist (G. P. Everett-Green) and a historian (Mary Anne Everett Wood), Evelyn Everett-Green's childhood was more academically oriented than that of most girls of her generation. She was educated at home until the age of 12, when she went to what she described as an 'intensively academic school', with the intention of going on to university. She did in fact win the Reid scholarship to Bedford College, and in an autobiographical piece for *The Silver Link* (January 1894) recalled her ambition on leaving school: 'I . . . had dreams of being a very erudite woman and learning everything under the sun. I had done well at school, especially in mathematics and Latin. I had dabbled in Greek on my own account, and was teaching myself Spanish.'[4]

College was initially disappointing, for she found the work too easy and had too much free time. At this point, Evelyn took to reading fiction, of which previously she had read very little, selecting, with her mother's guidance, 'poetry, history, and solid books'.[5] Her mother's disapproval of 'indiscriminate story-reading' was ignored, and the proximity of Mudie's to Bedford College proved an irresistible temptation. She not only took up reading fiction, but began to write it as well. While at Bedford she completed her first three-volume novel, *Oakhurst to Oxford*, which her sisters 'were ready to vow that "everybody would think a man had written"'.[6] She left Bedford College for the Royal Academy of Music, where the hours of practising left little time for writing, although she managed to prepare short stories for competitions and with these had some success.

Evelyn had intended to live with her favourite brother in India upon completing her education, but before this was possible he died, an event which profoundly affected her life. Her grief seems to have been mixed with guilt – possibly at not being with him; possibly at surviving him. In what appears to have been a kind of penance, she abandoned all her previous academic interests and concentrated on doing good works. At this point her public life became much more conventionally feminine in its round of duties and services. She visited the poor, taught in Sunday and night schools, and eventually trained to become a hospital nurse. At the same time, she began to have some success with her books for children.

These early works were not directed specifically at girls. Throughout her career Everett-Green wrote historical and moral tales for children of both sexes as well as her 'girls' stories', yet she became known primarily as a writer for girls. It appears that she realised that her books were being disparaged because her readers were both juvenile and female, and in 1909, at the age of 53, she adopted the pseudonym Cecil Adair, and subsequently produced two Adairs and one Everett-Green annually until her death. That Adair and Everett-Green were the same writer was known only by her publisher, Stanley Paul & Co., and the revelation caused a minor stir upon her death. *The Times* carried a second, enlarged, obituary for her (29 April 1932) in which the secret was revealed by a company director who raised the obvious question of why the Adair books were more successful than the Everett-Green.

There is indeed very little to choose between Cecil Adair and Evelyn Everett-Green and, as might be expected from so prodigious an *œuvre*, the quality of work varies considerably more from text to text than from 'author' to 'author'. It is tempting to suggest that her mainstream books were better written than those for girls, but there are some stupefyingly bad books in both categories as well as some perfectly adequate and, rarer, rather good pieces of writing.

It is impossible, and unnecessary, to give here a comprehensive survey of Evelyn Everett-Green's work. Because I am interested in her as a writer of girls' fiction, I have selected a small number of her girls' stories for analysis. My primary interest has been to see how this academically trained woman, who never married and was financially independent, responded to the pressures described in the previous chapter.

Her educational history suggests that Evelyn Everett-Green belonged to the category of Victorian girl-readers who consciously rejected girls' stories as feeble and enfeebling. They sought power and activity and therefore resisted being sucked into a reading position which constantly played upon the fact that they were different from boys, for the difference was always grounded in lack. They might be wiser, more virtuous and intellectually adept, but were unable to surpass their male cohort in the public arena. Those girls and women who did become powerful figures and about whose backgrounds we have some information seem universally to have sought to challenge the restrictions of their lot by approaching the world in an essentially masculine way: privileging rationality, reason and order. There were few critics of women's fiction more harsh than those women who determined to function in the male world of Victorian/Edwardian England. Florence Nightingale, George Eliot, Lillian Faithful (Headmistress of Cheltenham Ladies College), Beatrice Webb and Vera Brittain are among those who are on record as consciously rejecting feminine books for a reading regime based on male education. It might have been expected from her girlhood reading experiences that Evelyn Everett-Green would have numbered herself among such women readers. However, at roughly the time that her contemporaries would have been contemplating marriage, and when she seemed set to embark on an intellectual career, she rejected her mother's literary code and turned to the kind of books traditionally associated with women's reading.

It is not known why Evelyn never married. She was of the generation in which the unmarried 'odd women' were becoming increasingly common but which nevertheless maintained that a woman's true fulfilment came only through marriage and motherhood. It is possible that in not marrying she was rejecting this traditional attitude, but there is no evidence to support this belief in her writing. The bourgeois family underpins each story (even if one or both parents are absent because dead or posted to a climate unsuitable for children), and those with female heroines of marriageable age always conclude with a happy-ever-after union (and often a glimpse forward into the blisses of parenthood).

Evelyn Everett-Green had the academic training, the opportunity and, from what is known about her background, the family support to make her aware of the tensions and complexities surrounding the role and imaging of women in late nineteenth- and early twentieth-century Britain. It seems likely that she would have tried to inscribe some of the questions circulating around womanhood and femininity in her books. However, she was also attempting to support herself on the proceeds of her writing, and therefore could not afford to alienate publishers, parents and educators. She chose to write for children, and it may be that she felt that her audience precluded investigation of such issues, or that having established a money-making formula she was determined to adhere to it. For whatever reason, the fact remains that her books vigorously embrace and pass on traditional images of masculinity and femininity. If intended for a very young audience, the hero and heroine will be curly topped and lisping, but clearly he is manly and she is motherly. This treatment is typified in *Dickie and Dorrie at School*, in which Master Dickie has his babyish qualities rubbed off by playing football and learning the codes of the classroom, while Miss Dorrie finds her role ministering to the boys' bruises and cleaning out their gym lockers. Dickie proves himself able to handle the social complexities of school life, while Dorrie (who is staying with relatives rather than attending the school) alleviates spiritual problems. Dickie deals with arithmetic, thieves and liars, while Dorrie reforms the problem boy by loving him in the way she knows her mother would approve and nurses the sickly academic.

For the older reader the roles are no less plainly delineated (though the religious exegesis is noticeably diminished). In *Gladys or Gwenyth*, rich but unlovely Gwenyth shows how far service and self-sacrifice could go by bequeathing all her money to the beautiful but impoverished Gladys, much beloved of Sir Gerald, the man Gwenyth herself secretly loves. Sir Gerald, recently saddled with costly estates, has been unable to marry Gladys until Gwenyth's sudden death and unexpected bequest. Perhaps not surprisingly, the woman's roles as redeemer and giver are supreme in this mawkish tale, but even the dashing heroine of *A Wilful Maid* soon finds marriage and motherhood superior to the freedom and excitement she had enjoyed as a beautiful, wealthy, new-fashioned girl.

As a professional writer, Everett-Green may have decided that this was what public and publishers wanted, but there is nothing in the texts to suggest that she felt otherwise. Indeed, in her obituary her publisher observed that throughout her career she had remained, 'very much a Victorian, and kept a strict eye on the wrapper of her books', forbidding anything 'modern or indiscrete'.[7] In her study of women's recreational reading in the middle of the nineteenth century, Sally Mitchell provides some insights which may help to explain Everett-Green's writing and its reception. According to Mitchell, the novelist (and specifically the kind of low-status, popular, writer of sentimental/sensational fiction for women), 'does not create . . . emotions but gives . . . the codes to express existing emotional tensions, which are either formless because of decorum . . . or severely repressed because of social context.'[8] She later continues,

> The popular emotional novel gratifies common needs; it provides a mode of distancing which gives repressed emotions a form that is publically acceptable and makes them a source of pleasure. It also

affords recognition that these needs are common – shared between author and reader, reader and reader. The particular social situation within which author and reader live at any given time creates specific frustrations which cannot be resolved and must therefore have an outlet in fantasy. Furthermore, decorum differs from age to age; the things which have to be repressed, therefore, also differ. Thus, we should see popular novels as emotional analyses, rather than intellectual analyses, of a particular society.[9]

This identification of tension between reality (what you are to get) and desire (what you'd like to get) makes it possible to conclude that the predictable plots and endings were provided not because they reflected the real expectations of Everett-Green and her readers, but rather as a fantasy of how they wished their lives to be. The romantic heroines in her stories are relieved of anxiety about compromising their femininity by taking on jobs or operating in traditionally male spheres. There is nothing uncertain or innovative about their futures; all is comfortably familiar, predictable, safe and, better still, glossed over with the prospect of romantic love in the perfect union which endures forever in a soft-focus future. Her best novels for girls offered the possibility of enjoying vicariously the thrill of participating in emotional crises and the imaginative plea-sures arising from emotionally satisfying relationships and conclusions. Even when heroines had periods of excitement and activity, their behaviour never compromised the reader's sense of her own character or questioned the virtues and values in which she had been schooled. All her good qualities are recognised and rewarded and her bad ones excluded. Everett-Green's worst works are watered-down versions of the same formula, usually taking place in domestic settings.

Thus, just as in encouraging girls to see themselves as readers of fiction Meade may actually have prevented them from perceiving their real relations with the society in which they lived,[10] so Evelyn Everett-Green and writers like her provided a kind of placebo fiction which often seemed to offer challeng-ing settings and characters, but was in reality determined not to upset the existing social structure or to seek to acquire a more powerful independent, and so essentially 'masculine' way of functioning in the world. What is more, this type of fiction, with its strong adherence to the traditions of classic realism, seeks to draw in the reader in a way which has the potential to keep her from perceiving herself as independent.

A good example of the renunciation of power and independence is found in one of Everett-Green's best-known books, *Maud Melville's Marriage*. This is a historical tale and so by rights could be considered a book to be read by both sexes. However, as its title suggests, the central character is a girl and the plot and sub-plot are both romantic (indeed, the book ends by reminding readers that all of the action and the final happy ending were the result of 'that romantic Melville marriage'). For these reasons the book belongs to the girls' list and should be considered as the girls' equivalent of a Henty adventure.

Like Henty, Everett-Green attempts to instruct her readers about an historical event or period by creating a fictional character who lives through it. This story begins shortly after the coming to power of William and Mary, and is concerned with the political and social problems caused by religious intolerance following the vicissitudes of the Civil War, Protectorate and Restoration.

The plot revolves around the child-marriage of Rupert Melville and Lady Maud Wakefield, children of two neighbouring families (one Catholic and the other Protestant). Political expedience demands that Rupert and Maud be separated immediately after their marriage (which, youth aside, is portrayed as a love match). Maud spends the remainder of the book seeking for and finally saving her young husband, who has been unjustly jailed as a traitor. Having smuggled Rupert out of Newgate prison, Maud obtains a private audience with Queen Mary. The Queen, like a royal mother, comforts her, hears her troubles and gives the required pardon, telling Maud that she has been right to trust her instincts and to 'come to me to plead a wife's cause for an absent husband' (p. 302). The book ends with reconciliation between all members of the family and a new spirit of religious toleration and stability governing the land.

Lady Maud Melville's tale is told in part by a fictional narrator who claims to have found some old manuscripts, which form the basis of the story, in a family chest. The narrator fills in the gaps, but Lady Maud, who seems to have dictated her version of events to a relative, tells her own story for considerable portions of the book. The historical perspective achieved in this way, moving from a first-person account of past events to the present, is similar to that in Hawthorne's *The Scarlet Letter* when read with 'The Custom House'. The narrator is able to make comparisons between the seventeenth and nineteenth centuries, to provide lessons in history, politics, architecture and inventions, while the first-person account ensures interest and immediacy. The technique clearly demonstrates the post-Darwinian tendency to use the past to explain the present and the understanding that history is never an accurate reconstruction of the past but a more or less fictional account of events as they are understood in the present.

Maud Melville's Marriage is a good example of the kind of book which may be dismissed as a 'girls' story', yet which in many ways conforms to the conventions of the best boys' books. It is as full of action, intrigue and historical detail as any Henty. Although the battlegrounds tend to be personal rather than military, there are many references to actual battles and rebellions. Through occasional asides Everett-Green incorporates the familiar link between masculinity and patriotism. A good example of this is provided by Maud's Uncle Fells, who refused to leave London when the plague was at its worst. He could easily have stepped out of the pages of one of Henty's books: 'Mr Fells was one of those tough, determined men who despise a panic, and who had the true British instinct of standing to his post at all costs.' (p. 139)

There are many fine male characters in *Maud Melville's Marriage*, but an equal number of fools and bigots. Although it is men who generate all of the social and political affairs which give rise to the plot, it is actually the female characters who preserve values and bring about resolution and reforms. Maud's mother was the hidden strength in the Wakefield household. She refused to become involved at court and spent her time bringing up children and doing good work for the poor. It is largely through her council and actions that the family manages to survive the long knives of the politicians in the turbulent period which precedes the action of the book. Maud's mother teaches her that as a woman and a Christian, whatever her lot, her life need never be empty or sorrowful. It is this philosophy which leads Maud to take up prison visiting, find her husband and secure their future happiness.

There are other good and influential women in the book, the most important of whom is the Queen. Maud's plea is effective because she avoids politics and speaks about her love as one wife to another, yet she is only able to achieve her purpose (the granting of an official pardon) because the King is away and in his absence the Queen's signature sufficed for the joint mandate (p. 304).

Maud's impassioned outburst to the Queen is totally out of character. Previously she had been noted for being articulate and self-contained. In these qualities she is shown to be atypical and different from her passive, passionless and uninformed sisters. By contrast Maud,

> had loved books and learning from a chid, and her quick, precocious intelligence had been awakened and deepened by the peculiar circumstances that surrounded her own life. She possessed opinions and views of her own. She was little disposed to submit tamely to her brother's rule. Dutiful towards her parents, and devoted as she had ever been to her mother, she had a strong will, a strong nature, and an ingrained spirit of courageous independence not easily daunted. (p. 82)

The disparaging description of Maud's sisters and the presentation of real female power (i.e. the Queen) make it tempting to try to read at least this one of Evelyn Everett-Green's works as encoding a covert but consistent challenge to male authority. Through the principal female characters, she seems to suggest that while women operated less conspicuously than men, at least when will, education and class were conjoined, their influence was considerable. Moreover, she contrasts male power struggles, bellicosity and the political turmoil they engendered with a view of female patience, toleration, vision and a capacity for immediate, positive, action in a way which suggests that women are more capable and effective at what they do than are men.

What does this comparison actually mean within the text? There are two principal ways of approaching this question. The first is to join those feminists who criticise women writers of sentimental fiction as propagandists for a degenerate social system, encouraging 'anti-intellectual consumerism, the rationalisation of an unjust economic order, the propagation of the debased images of modern mass culture and the encouragement of self-indulgence and narcissim in literature's most avid readers – women'.[11] Any protests which seem to be directed against social policy and practice are construed as phantasms because such writers, being damaged victims of oppression, and their dishonesty of a kind 'for which there is no known substitute in a capitalist country' neither desire change nor believe it will occur.[12]

An alternative interpretation is that sentimental women's fiction was not produced by women whose political consciousness had failed them, but was in fact highly political as it provided a sustained emotional attack on male-dominated western society and, through the discourse of sacrifice and salvation, replaced it with a matriarchy.[13] This approach is optimistic rather than accurate, and is weakened by the fact that the discourses which it says are supposed to empower women (Christianity, self-sacrifice and purification) are precisely those which have been used to control them.

The accuracy of a reading which sees women's power inscribed in their fiction may be debatable, but it is a comforting mythology for those who chafed against their real inability to act. This interpretation is important for it suggests that women's fiction provides its readers with a sense of power and self-esteem which depends on their not attempting to challenge the existing social order. Thus it does not necessarily describe a power-structure in which women readers believed themselves to be operating, but one in which they wished to see themselves. As Mitchell points out, the fictional solution further comforts readers by tacitly acknowledging that their frustrations and fantasies are shared. This, rather than a desire to subvert patriarchy, is the attitude which informs the writing of Evelyn Everett-Green, for while condemning short-sighted and polarised male leaders, at no point does she challenge the patriarchal system of either seventeenth or nineteenth century Britain. Indeed, *Maud Melville's Marriage* can be seen as an affirmation of the separation of male and female spheres of work, duty and influence. Maud, like her mother and the Queen, is effective because she never seeks to trespass into male preserves. She knows her place and so is able to cleanse and inspire the men with whom she is in contact. She is her mother's daughter, and like that paragon, 'a good wife, a tender mother, and a far-seeing woman; and she was very well convinced [of the need] to submit . . . to the will of the husband she had vowed to love, honour, and obey.' (p. 28)

The structure of *Maud Melville's Marriage* and its imaging of women are essentially conservative. The plot summary shows the affective qualities of the narrative; it is slightly more difficult to characterise the language. The reason for the difficulty is located in the historical nature of the text and Everett-Green's concern with illustrating the increasing pace of change over the past two hundred years.

The contrast between past and present permeates the novel, but because change is presented as organic and gradual it does not engender confusion or negative responses such as anxiety or resistance. This illustrates how the language in a work such as *Maud Melville's Marriage* corresponds to Bakhtin's domain of the classical body. It presupposes an educated and proficient reader as evidenced by its vocabulary, which is varied and quite sophisticated, and prose which is often syntactically complex. Both language and content are consciously didactic and el-evated. While sophisticated, complex writing certainly lends itself more readily to heteroglossic than monoglossic language, Everett-Green eschews writing which draws attention to multiple meanings and conflict. Just as the plot upholds the authority of the state, institutions, fathers and husbands, so the language respects the conventions of standard English. There are no buffoons to introduce uncouth dialects or subjects, and effectively no point at which rogue elements might find entrance. For instance, when Maud is told about low life in London, it is as part of a lecture on architecture and morality delivered in the measured and educated phraseology of her Uncle Fells. Even her servant, Gowrie, speaks correctly and is a noble woman. Furthermore, as an author Everett-Green is content to recycle language and never attempts to force meaning through stylistic improvisations. Neither is she using conflicting languages to represent the conflicts taking place in her society. Rather, Everett-Green's books create an illusion of harmony and unity.

The monoglossic nature of *Maud Melville's Marriage* is typical of Evelyn Everett-Green's writing. Even the slang of the dashing Lady Angela Goldhawk, heroine of *A Wilful Maid*, is made acceptable by the monoglossic drive of the narrative. Lady Angela is a 'new-fashioned' girl. Initially described as both 'graceful' and 'rather boyish-looking', she is one of the many reformed tomboys of late-Victorian and Edwardian girls' fiction.

That Everett-Green was not in favour of the behaviour of 'girls of the period' is rapidly apparent in *A Wilful Maid*. Once in contact with a 'proper' man, Lady Angela rapidly changes from the boyish-looking girl to a thoroughly feminine young woman. Indeed, one of her first conversations with her future husband, Hugh Constable, shows the change has already begun. Lady Angela empathises with Hugh's frustration at the inertia imposed upon him by his need to convalesce after an accident saying, 'I just know how you must hate not being able to do things. I'm like that myself. I always think I was meant to be a man.' To which Hugh replies, 'I do not feel that at all . . . I don't think you are in the least masculine in mind, body, or estate!' (p. 192)

Hugh cancels Angela's desire to have the power and freedom of a man by emphasising her innate femininity and, in the process, signals that whatever doubt the reader may have had about her up to now, Lady Angela is going to be saved for the domestic altar by the end of the book. Her capitulation is as much a part of the reformed-tomboy convention as are the discontented speeches she makes to Hugh during their courtship. Everett-Green has Lady Angela question the role of women in society:

> Oh, to be a man – one of the men who have lives to live! . . . . Why aren't we allowed to choose for ourselves? It's a shame to give a woman strength and health, and all the desire after adventure and glory, and then to coop her up to a silly frivolous life where she hasn't even a vote to use! (p. 267)

These familiar arguments are answered within the plot when it transpires that Lady Angela has, through an unfortunate escapade in which she did not appreciate the powers of language, enabled herself to be blackmailed by a man who claims that according to Scottish law she is his wife. Her secret is finally revealed (and the rogue exposed as an adulterer and con man); Everett-Green presents the event as the inevitable outcome of slipshod modern speech and loose ways, and thereby advocates a return to traditional feminine behaviour. Lady Angela's godmother, Miss Goldhawk, tells her that her ordeal

> is the price you modern girls sometimes have to pay for your harum-scarum ways. You find yourselves placed in false positions, which would have been avoided entirely had you exercised a little more of that decorum and reserve which in the days of your mothers was taken as a matter of course. (p. 322)

Hugh, who like Miss Goldhawk is associated with traditional values and behaviour, but who also has the persuasive qualities of the romantic hero, points out the responsibilities of freedom and tacitly criticises the fast set in which his future wife has previously been a leading member: 'I think that modern life ought to make girls and women more discriminating. They see and hear a great deal that their grandmothers never did. And they do not grow up with the idea that marriage is the only goal of life.' (p. 194)

Thus in *A Wilful Maid*, as in many of her other books, Everett-Green discouraged her readers from succumbing to the novelties and immediate pleasures on offer to the modern young woman and came down in favour of what were represented as the tried and proven gratifications of previous generations.

Many feminist critics have worked on the assumption that nineteenth-century women writers of adult poetry and fiction were attempting to reshape the male literary tradition to suit their own needs, but their observations do not hold true for women, such as Evelyn Everett-Green and L. T. Meade, who wrote girls' fiction of roughly the same period.[14] Repression does not seem to have provoked invention; neither are there identifiable dissenting or questioning voices in these works. The reason for this seems to be simply that girls' fiction is not part of the male literary tradition. Though edited, published and marketed by men, the writing is separate and designated (largely by the controlling men) the preserve of female readers. It appears to have been decided in advance that the readers of such books are not interested in (or should be protected from) intellectual analysis, but do enjoy an emotional exegesis. Understanding the marketing policy behind such writing makes it less surprising that girls' fiction consistently excluded both events and discourses which sought to challenge the status quo. That this is the case becomes even more apparent in the following brief survey of popular fiction books for girls written in late-Victorian and Edwardian England.

What Katy Did

One of the most interesting phenomena to emerge from a study of late-Victorian and Edwardian fiction for girls is authors' recurrent use of temporary paralysis to bring about the reform of the central 'rebel' character. The bold, verbally precocious, challenging, and therefore 'bad' (in terms of the feminine ideal) heroine is, as the result of an accident or emotional crisis, led to enlightenment and converted into the perfect domestic angel.

The effect of the crisis is to simulate an infantile state of dependency and confusion. The heroine effectively becomes a very young girl again and, having lost or unlearned the mistaken codes by which she had been operating (e.g. those based on qualities designated masculine: independence, aggression, intellectual curiosity), she relearns how to conduct herself in society. This means relinquishing usurped masculine behaviour and discourse – in Lacan's terms abandoning the urge to master the Symbolic order. Her first attempt at social dialogue has, as it were, been mispronounced and her grammar found faulty. When she returns to the world, all is corrected. The new, old-fashioned model speaks in reformed language and modulated tones. Her behaviour is moderated, her aspirations ·scaled down. No longer a radiant being, fearless of rejection and crammed full of liberated zest and ideals (which from experience the reader knows are doomed to end in disaster) she is now capable of being fulfilled by the conventional life likely to be her lot.

This pattern of events is significant for two reasons. First, the state of confusion following unorthodox childhood is often thought to be characteristic of adolescence, while the learning of language and acceptable behaviour is part of the experience of every social being. The structure thus establishes a situation likely to correspond to that of the young reader and allows her to become involved in the resolution of conflict and the promise of fulfilment in the traditional role.

The structural device of regression, reintroduction to the Symbolic order (with its connotations of sexual difference) and reform is reinforced by the narrative's assumption that the reader shares the attitudes and values which inform the text. Instead of exploring the contradictions and frustrations inherent in the lives of young women because they lack power, wealth, and autonomy, these works coerce the reader into anticipating and desiring conformity for the heroine because it offers the only successful means of resolving crises and permitting a happy ending. The authorial position is never evasive, but does its best to ensure that the reader is clear about, and accepts, the moral and social messages in the text. Social life which adheres to the dominant ideological construction of femininity emerges as solid, safe and satisfying; individual resistance as precarious, mad, and destructive. This combination of patterning and perspective is clearly at work in one of the most successful examples of the new girl's fiction, Susan Coolidge's *What Katy Did* (1870).

When wild, unconventional Katy Carr, whose ambitions include studying and becoming famous, disobeys her aunt and takes a forbidden swing, a staple breaks away and she falls to the ground, damaging her spine. So begins Katy's period of dependency as a preliminary to re-entering the world according to accepted social forms:

> . . . there came a time when Katy didn't even ask to be allowed to get up . . . when sharp, dreadful pain, such as she never imagined before, took hold of her. Her days and nights got all confused and tangled up together. . . . It was all like a long, bad dream.
>
> (pp. 155–6)

After four weeks of delirium, Katy experiences a second infancy physically, 'the once active limbs hung heavy and lifeless, and she was not able to walk or even stand alone.' (p. 158) Forced to accept that she is likely to be physically dependent for ever, Katy is more subtly encouraged to mould her mind to the constrictions of womanly ways. Her invalid cousin, Helen, instructs her in the 'school of pain', the lessons of which are patience, cheerfulness, making the best of things, hopefulness and neatness. Significantly, when Katy warms to Helen's influence, her attempts at relearning social behaviour are presented in the form of a dream based on the acquisition of language:

> She thought she was trying to study a lesson out of a book which she couldn't quite open. She could just see a little bit of what was inside, but it was in a language which she did not understand. She tried in vain; not a word could she read.
>
> (p. 177)

As the dream-Katy proves her repentance and earnestness, the task is suddenly made easy, for the guiding hand of 'the

Teacher' opens the book and points to each phrase. As she steps on to the well-trodden path of femininity, with its familiar Christian signposts, Katy discovers that she can read the lines without difficulty.

The efficacy of Cousin Helen's lesson concludes *What Katy Did*, for when the paralysis leaves her, Katy has been transformed from a wilful tomboy likely to become a 'girl of the period', into the domestic angel she earlier scorned. Cousin Helen comes to celebrate Katy's recovery and tells her:

> . . . how pleased I am to see how bravely you have worked your way up. I can perceive in everything – in papa, the children, in yourself. You have won the place which . . . I once told you an invalid should try to gain, of being to everybody, 'the Heart of the House'. (p. 255)

For Victorian women, surrounded as they were by invalids, Katy's months in bed operate as both a symbolic reliving of infancy and the trauma engendered by taking up a sexual identity, and as a prefiguring of adult life.

The theme of self-denial and its reward is typical of the girls' books which flourished after 1880 and persists into the twentieth century. Each of these young women starts by demonstrating unconventional behaviour, then makes one grand act or gesture of abnegation which prepares her for assuming the halo and robes of the domestic angel. This theme is frequently underlined by L. T. Meade. In her highly popular *A Sister of the Red Cross* (1901), Meade attacks outright women who wish to reject their positions and duties in the home for careers and the freedoms they entail. The father of one such progressive young woman upbraids her in speech which encapsulates the whole conservative argument:

> You think you are doing your duty. You are very – painfully – modern. The old ideas with regard to 'Honour thy father and mother' are exploded in this end of the nineteenth century. It is a dull sort of task to stay at home with an old man, and it is heroic, and glorious, and grand to step out of your place and go where God

knows you may not be wanted. . . . It is a mistaken idea of duty, according to my way of thinking.   (p. 184)

In other words, girls are to give up modern notions of independence and accept the heroism of lives of domestic service and parental obedience. Interestingly, the accusation levelled here against the activities and aspirations of middle-class girls is precisely the same as that being levelled at working women in the industrial centres at this time. Women who went to work, it was argued, failed in their foremost duty to family and society by creating conditions for moral decay through deficient patterns of family life.[15] The propaganda against working women was so effective that the exclusion of women from the labour forces became bound up with notions of respectability and manhood.[16] By the end of the century, a Ruskinian ideal of women's role had been so effectively promoted that there was a widespread retreat into the home on the part of working-class women.[17] Women's role at home, holding the family together during a period of rapid social transition, was advertised as pivotal and both her obligation and source of power.

The new girls' fiction regularly employs the same ideological strategy. By following the trials and progress of the 'naughty' heroines, girl readers learn to appreciate the family which both protects them and provides the opportunity for service, self-sacrifice and the preparation for wifely duties. The books remind girls to be grateful for parents' guidance, which keeps them from moral lapses and inappropriate behaviour. They cast a jaundiced eye over what they suggest are the temporary, superficial and questionable attractions of the new woman, and celebrate instead the old domestic ideal.

Like the stories of Everett-Green, these examples, and those which follow, show how girls' fiction facilitated the suppression of changes in the imaging of women by providing an outlet in which real-life anxieties and contradictions could be confronted and contained. As each of the texts moves towards closure, conflicts and tensions are harmoniously resolved by rejecting struggle and opposition for conventional behaviour. With renunciation, the books promise, comes fulfilment.

The books have a narcotic quality; at first they arouse unaccustomed and exciting feelings by encouraging sympathy for the rebellious heroines, thereby providing vicarious experience and the release that goes with it. They then damp down the excitement and dull the senses by offering resolutions which 'prove' that the known and familiar is, after all, the best and most enjoyable.

A similar mechanism, which encouraged women to participate in their own regulation and restriction by limiting what they perceived as appropriate goals and behaviours, was the implantation of a value construct centred on traditional notions of femininity. Recent work on female oppression examines the way in which the existence of a normative ideal of what constitutes a socially attractive and successful woman operates to cause women to adhere to its values and restrict themselves accordingly.[18] It is possible to see the value construct surrounding images of 'the lady' and the 'womanly' woman at work informing and diverting the course of female education and its representation in books for girls through the girls' school story.

L. T. Meade's girls' school stories

No matter how thoroughly girls' stories reject changes in the imaging and status of women, it is undeniable that fundamental changes were taking place in the opportunities available to young women. Perhaps most significant of these was the change in attitude to girls' education and the alterations in regulation it entailed.

Charlotte M. Yonge was typical in her thinking about women's education for most of the century. She believed that girls should be educated at home, and that their most important lesson was in 'self-control'. Handbooks for parents and medical treatises on adolescent girls consistently emphasised the necessity of surveillance, regulation and, particularly, the avoidance of boarding schools for pubescent girls.[19] Young ladies were confined and controlled to keep them from imbibing unofficial sexual knowledge which, it was believed, would convert a girl's desires into a 'devouring flame, and onanism'.[20]

In spite of these dire warnings and a well-developed suspicion of schools for girls, by the end of the century higher education for women was becoming a social fact and offered much-needed training for the increasing number of women who were required to earn their own living. Indeed, by the last two decades of the nineteenth century a developed intellect came to be regarded as an asset for a woman, either because it helped her attract a husband or enabled her to provide for herself if she failed to get married. More and more girls underwent some kind of further education with the proviso that their training also helped to prepare them for running a household.

The pressure to make education consistent with femininity led to the incorporation of domestic science and household management into the curricula of many girls' colleges. The comfort this afforded parents and the emphasis given to it over academic subjects is reflected in a letter received by Miss Molly Lavender, the central character in L. T. Meade's *Girls New and Old* (1896). Molly has reported that her Principal believes that in addition to academic subjects, a girl must know how to use her hands, to cook, and be knowledgeable in all branches of housework. 'All this knowledge,' she tells Molly, 'is a great and wonderful possession.' (p. 38)

Molly's father receives this information with enthusiasm and replies:

Miss Forester must be a remarkable woman . . . I don't especially care for learned women. I like a girl to be thoroughly and well domesticated, and to think no household work beneath her knowledge. . . . I am easily pleased. . . . A little clear soup nicely flavoured, a cutlet done to a turn, with the correct sauce . . . a savoury omelette, a *meringue* or jelly, makes up the simple dinner which more than satisfies your affectionate father. You will think

this a trifling matter, my darling, when you are perusing your Latin
or Greek, and those other abstruse subjects which are now
considered essential to the feminine mind. . . . Whatever you do,
Molly, strive to retain all the gentle privileges of your sex . . . and to
acquire those nice accomplishments which are essential to the
comfort of man.   (pp. 49–52)

Molly Lavender is, in fact, a manageable, old-fashioned girl
never likely to stray from the conventional path (a fact signalled
by what is referred to as her 'dear little rustic English' name.
Upon meeting her the Principal predicts:

Molly Lavender is just the sort of girl who will make a splendid
woman by-and-by. . . . She is not especially clever, but she is
capable and lovable; she is just the sort of womanly girl who will
help on the cause of the New Woman in the most effective way; she
will take up all the best of the movement, and leave the bad alone.
                                                              (p. 296)

By which it is meant that Molly will adapt to altered circumstances without deviating from the ideological ambition to
designate her qualities of self-effacement and denial positive
social virtues.

Girls New and Old is typical of girls' stories at the end of the
century in its acknowledgement that the stage for girls and the
kinds of opportunities before them had changed. Higher
education and the necessity for some women to be able to
support themselves are facts in these books, but carefully
prevented from challenging the idealised social construction of
the domestic angel. Through an inversion of genius, the school
setting which had seemed so threatening is, in this new off-shoot
of girls' fiction, turned upon itself and made the means of new
and greater opportunities for self-denial, service and adherence
to the established principles of femininity. At the same time, the
works subtly instil a model and code of internal self-regulation
which had to replace the old, external parental and social
controls once girls no longer received their educations and
preparation for the world exclusively at home. Both methods of

supporting the old ideal are at work in L. T. Meade's *A Sweet Girl Graduate* (1891).

This is the story of Priscilla Penywren Peel, oldest of four orphaned sisters in the care of their poor and aged aunt. Priscilla has been educated by the local clergyman, who recognises that she is clever and urges the aunt to send her to college where she can be trained to earn her own living and support her siblings. This is done with the utmost scrimping and saving. Priscilla arrives at the gates of St. Benet's College badly outfitted, anxious about money and with her aunt's parting words ringing in her ears: 'I don't hold with the present craze about women's education. But I feel somehow I shall be proud of you. You'll be learned enough, but you'll be a woman with it all.' (p. 9) Thus, from the outset, Priscilla must reconcile two conflicting roles – the intellectual young lady who needs to be financially independent, and the womanly woman. Like many girls of the time, Priscilla leaves the confines and controls of family life for a world in which external regulation seems to be minimised.

The reader learns along with Priscilla that, 'A girl's life at one of the women's colleges is supposed to be more or less an unfettered sort of existence; the broad rules guiding conduct are few.' (p. 20) Regulation has not exactly disappeared, however, but instead has changed its *modus operandi*: 'There was a regularity and yet a freedom about the life; invisible bounds were prescribed, beyond which no right-minded or conscientious girl cared to venture, but the rules were really very few.' (p. 34) The Headmistress describes the situation thus: 'There are no punishments. Up to a certain point [a girl] is free to be industrious or not as she pleases. Some rules there are for her conduct and guidance, but they are neither many nor arbitrary.' (p. 105)

It soon becomes clear that the girls are judicious and exacting in their self-imposed regulation. Organised around the principles of what makes 'a nice young lady' are a number of unwritten but understood codes. Priscilla learns of their existence on her first evening at college, when shyness and rusticity combine to make her unintentionally blind to expected behaviour. The brilliant and popular Miss Maggie

Oliphant takes the new girl under her wing and explains the situation: 'We are supposed to be very democratic and go in for all that is advanced in womanhood. But, oh dear, oh dear! let any student dare to break one of our own little pet proprieties, and you will soon see how conservative we can be.' (p. 22)

The two girls become firm friends. Maggie's wealth, advanced ideas and wit are tempered by womanly attributes. Her personality is reflected in the cosy room she has made for herself, where books and music are subsumed by the domestic comforts of ornaments, a glowing fire and a kettle always singing merrily on the hob. Priscilla had been educated according to the boys' curriculum remembered by the clergyman from his own schooldays. Consequently, she has developed a taste for the classics which she shares with Maggie. In the semiotics of these texts, this delight in antique languages is indicative of a precarious state of femininity. A knowledge of Greek and Latin was not consistent with being a well-brought-up young woman, for it was believed that familiarity with the classics would introduce a girl to unseemly knowledge of the classical world, with its explorations of sexual licentiousness, including homosexual love and violence.

That Meade supports this orthodoxy is made clear as the story reaches its climax. Priscilla's family's poverty becomes desperate when her aged aunt falls ill and cannot work. Priscilla, who is acknowleged to be a brilliant scholar, determines to abandon studying Greek and Latin and to concentrate on modern languages, which will be of more use to her when she is earning her living. Maggie Oliphant offers her friend sufficient funds to maintain her family and make it possible for Priscilla to continue studying for the tripos. After a struggle, Priscilla turns down the offer and the likelihood of a first class degree. Her headmistress approves of the decision, telling Maggie that her friend will win herself a golden crown, more precious than the one of bay her intellect might have won. She says:

I have never admired Priscilla more. . . . I encouraged her to give up her classics . . . to devote herself to modern languages, and to those accomplishments which are considered more essentially feminine.

As I did so, I had a picture before me, in which I saw Priscilla crowned with love; the support and blessing of her three little sisters. (p. 281)

The book thunders to a close in a celebration of self-renunciation and femininity:

Everyone prophesied well for Priscilla in the future which lay before her; her feet were set in the right direction; the aim of her life was to become – not learned, but wise; not to build up a reputation, but to gain character; to put blessedness before happiness – duty before inclination. (p. 207)

Thus, in the character of Priscilla Penywren Peel are harmonised the conflicting roles demanded of girls in late-Victorian and Edwardian England. Her intellectual capabilities have been recognised and given licence before being abandoned or repressed for the life of great and true fulfilment. She is, we are told, the kind of woman who 'lives at the root of the true life of a worthy nation'. (p. 288)

A Sweet Girl Graduate shows how girls' fiction reconciled changes in life-style and new opportunities for girls with the existing definition of femininity. The rapid changes in girls' lives gave rise to a literature which encouraged its readers to believe that they could move with the times and could modify their behaviour without departing from traditional expectations. More importantly, just as the introduction of New Women in the adult novel helped to accustom the public to social change in women's roles, so these reformed rebels not only revitalised the domestic angel in books for girls, but in the process, created an audience which colluded in its own containment and a reader who reacted against change, adhering to – or even reverting to – her place in the home and a moral ambience based on feminine idealism.

The Girl's Own Paper – *facts and fiction*

Its good work is unbounded. Probably the best feature of the paper is its prize competitions. These are made the medium of charity.

For instance, in 1885, 700 mufflers and 1,224 pairs of cuffs sent in in competitions were presented to occupants of London workhouses . . . subscribers to the *Girl's Own Paper* raised among themselves £1,000 towards establishing a 'Girl's Own Home' for the benefit of underpaid London girls of the working classes . . . the *Girl's Own* numbers among its contributors many famous ladies and gentle-men, but its great merit is that it does not depend entirely on fiction for its success, but gives interesting articles on all kinds of household matters.

(Edward J. Salmon, 'What girls read', 1886)

A year after the successful launch of the *Boy's Own Paper*, the Religious Tract Society brought forth a sister periodical, the *Girl's Own Paper*. Also priced at an affordable one penny, the *GOP* was initially a slightly shorter magazine, formatted for fourteen pages instead of the *BOP*'s usual sixteen. Apart from this obvious physical difference (which lasted only briefly), superficially the content of the girls' paper was not dissimilar to that of its male counterpart. It too combined 'healthy fiction' (e.g. that characterised by Christian morality and not excessive-ly fanciful) with informative articles and practical tips. The end product, however, was actually very different. Where the *BOP*'s fiction emphasised activity, independence and the triumph of muscle and mind over adverse conditions, that in the *GOP* was primarily concerned with affective relationships and domestic scenarios. While boys read about scientific inventions, how to make machines and survival in the tropics, girls were given recipes for furniture and face creams, patterns for needlework and features on the domestic lives of girls in foreign lands. Their spheres of interest were as different as their (male) editors' ambitions. G. A. Hutchinson sought to estab-lish the *BOP* as a high-status publication with contributors who were eminent in their fields and fiction renowned for its literary quality. Charles Peters (who edited the *GOP* from 1879–1907) described the goals of his journal in the prospectus of 1880: 'This magazine will aim at being to the girls a Counsellor, Playmate, Guardian, Instructor, Companion and Friend. It will help to train them in moral and domestic virtues, preparing them for the responsibilities of womanhood and for a heavenly home.'[21]

The most important difference between the *BOP* and the *GOP* lies in the deliberately eclectic nature of the girls' magazine and the ambiguity at the heart of its presentation of girlhood and femininity. By contrast, the *BOP* had a clear concept of its audience and what it wanted to achieve. This division can be understood in terms of Rousseau's formulation of sexual difference, to which the Victorian concept of 'separate spheres' for men and women owed much. This model presented men as possessing virtually unlimited potential for rationality and abstract thought, and women as sensual, irrational, and incapable of abstracting.[22] Femininity was presented as the inferior counterpart of masculinity in a model which did not separate gender from biological sex.

While this version of masculinity seems to have gone more or less unchallenged in juvenile publications of this period, there were several attempts to resist the one-sided view of femininity in books and periodicals directed at girls (indeed, it could be argued that the more the girls' publications sought to change the image of femininity, the more the boys' insisted on their readers' innate supremacy and exaggerated the characteristics on which it was based). The better girls' papers never ignored the sensual and emotional needs of their readers, but they also attempted to cultivate their rationality. Girls were encouraged to respect their own capabilities and to assume responsibility for developing their minds and skills. The *GOP*, in particular, sought to reform the attitudes and policies which kept girls financially dependent and so often reduced them to a kind of invisible slavery. Yet precisely the kind of ambivalence which kept Miss Buss reading *The Angel in the House* to her students each morning characterised the *Girl's Own Paper*. Girls were not incited to reject traditional feminine characteristics; purity, obedience, dependence, self-sacrifice and service are all presented as desirable qualities for the magazine's readers. However, the image of feminine womanhood was expanded to incorporate intelligence, self-respect and, when necessary, the potential to become financially independent. Thus it is possible

to see articulated in this early periodical the kind of contradictory tendencies characteristic of femininity: reason and desire,
autonomy and dependent activity, psychic and social
identity.[23]

This circulation of terms, positions and practices is particularly evident in the contrast between the fiction and non-fiction
features of the magazine. The non-fiction items frequently
encouraged girls to learn skills and prepare to be independent,
while the fiction, with its combination of romantic plots in
domestic settings, enabled them to act out psychic conflicts and
to assume discursive reading positions which encouraged them
to accept the existing power structure. (Today girls' fiction
continues to make great use of catharsis.[24]) Perhaps because of
the crudeness of this division, the *Girl's Own Paper* has not
found favour with contemporary critics. Carpenter and
Prichard (1984) describe the *GOP* as the 'less robust companion to the *BOP*, featuring, 'duteous behaviour and homemak-
ing skills'.[25] Cadogan and Craig (1976) also compare it un-
favourably with the *BOP* and describe it as consisting of
'domestic fiction, rather drab school stories and gentle anec-
dotes about the childhood of Queen Victoria'.[26] I find it
difficult to describe as drab or lacking in robustness a paper
which can juxtapose articles on how to take and develop your
own photographs, graphic exposures of child cruelty and the
atrocious working conditions of London's poorest girls, how
to have 'lissom hands and pretty feet', learning to play the
piano, poultry keeping and female heroism. There is certainly
nothing insipid in its handling of readers, either, as the
following reply to a correspondent shows:

ABRUPT – We cannot give you any recipe for making your hair
grow dark, nor any for 'getting rid of a double chin'. Be thankful
that you have got any hair or chin at all, and that the hair you
complain of does not grow on your chin.   (1888–9)

It seems likely that the disparaging remarks of critics stem
largely from the tendency to regard publications directed at
girls as inferior to those aimed at boys. Significantly, Edward

141

Salmon's praise of the paper is based upon a notion of what was appropriate in a *girl*'s magazine – in particular, its good works – rather than its literary merit. High status in this sense was not among Charles Peters' concerns. This is not to imply that the magazine was in any sense 'downmarket', but only that it did not set itself up to be an intellectual forum. For instance, instead of advertising the expertise of its contributors, the *GOP* emphasised their social status and/or pedigrees – many of the features were supplied by princesses, countesses and baronesses.

Whatever modern taste makes of the original *Girl's Own Paper*, in its day it was undeniably popular. Its circulation rose rapidly and soon surpassed that of the *BOP*, making it the largest-selling illustrated paper in the land.[27] This fact is hardly surprising: as the editor pointed out to a correspondent, the paper set out to appeal to a wide readership.

> Anyone, with half an eye, can see that the 'GOP' is intended for girls of all classes. Girls of a superior position – belonging, we mean, to the 'upper ten thousand' – should read everything, and be well up in *every* matter upon which we give instruction. Their money, time, and superior intelligence admit of this. For girls of a less high position there are papers on economical cookery, plain needlework, home education, and health. Servant-maids communicate to us well-written letters, and by their tone we can see that our magazine has indeed helped them to an intelligent carrying out of their humble work; that it has been a companion to them in their isolation and a counsellor in times of sore temptation. There is much in our paper we humbly believe that will train these girls in living a pure and honest life, and we rejoice to help them, for their letters convince us that there is honesty and nobility even in the kitchen. From our daily letters from the girls, written upon coronetted notepaper by those of noble birth, and by others from the kitchens of humble houses, we gather that there is help needed by all, and that our paper has given a high aim to their lives and a practical and wise assistance in their various engagements.[28]

The *Girl's Own Paper* tried not only to appeal to readers of all classes, but also to 'girls' of all ages. The *Girl's Own Paper* was never entirely clear as to what was meant by the word 'girl'. Competitions were restricted to those under the age of 25, but girls as young as six corresponded with the editor, as did those of middle and late years. This wide appeal was primarily achieved through the non-fiction pages, which outnumbered those devoted to stories and poems. They ranged from articles on cruelty to children, to teach-yourself foreign languages, travel features and domestic hints. The household sections on cookery, needlework, the care of furniture and children, together with instruction on domestic economy and careers advice, were in 1930 hived off to form a separate women's magazine. From a contemporary perspective it may seem odd to find fiction which is primarily concerned with the lives, loves and domestic duties of youthful heroines side-by-side with features on gardening, managing servants, the treatment of childhood ills, and 'How I keep house on £250 a year'. For the girl growing up in late-Victorian and Edwardian England, however, the blend made considerably more sense. It is by understanding the nature of this appeal that I think it is possible to gain further insights into the role played by the juvenile publishing industry in the formation of notions of sexual difference.

The pressure on girls to put childhood behind them and become womanly which such a mixture implies is not in fact unique to the late-Victorian and Edwardian period. Valerie Walkerdine's recent study of subjectivity class and gender in contemporary schooling shows a similar trend. Girls today, she concludes, are still discouraged from taking on active roles, and specifically from speaking publicly, because they understand such behaviour to be unfeminine.[29] Furthermore, she asserts that female childhood continues to be unstable, just as it was for the girl/women readers of the *GOP*: 'By definition, active childhood and passive femininity exist at the intersection of competing discourses. For girls, therefore, their positions as children must remain shaky and partial, continually played across by their position as feminine.'[30]

Perhaps because of historical distance, this girl/woman reader is more readily explained as a product of Victorian/

Edwardian society which believed that middle-class girls should be taught as early as possible to become good wives and mothers. While their brothers had considerably more time and freedom for 'just being boys' (though this in itself was no easy task, as I have pointed out), girls were steadily guided towards young womanhood. In poorer families they helped with all of the domestic chores – a practical preparation for going into service when the time came. Girls whose families were better off had endless fancy work to complete interspersed with lessons in music, dancing, French or other suitable accomplishments. There were visits to be paid and received, dresses to be fitted, meals to be ordered, the poor to be visited and a whole host of similar activities. Even the girl who was caught up in the new vogue for fresh air and exercise for young ladies had soon enough to leave such activities behind with her schooldays and, like H. G. Wells' Ann Veronica, to occupy herself as best she could in 'a functionless existence varied by calls, tennis, selected novels, walks and dusting in her father's house'.[31]

The first volume of the *Girl's Own Paper* addressed itself to precisely this problem in an article titled 'Between school and marriage'. It begins, 'this time in a girl's life corresponds to that in a man's which is passed in university, or in learning the work of his profession.' The author encourages girls from poorer families to have no qualms about earning their own livings – a stance the magazine always supported. The better off receive quite different advice: when the family has sufficient means, the girl ought to

> let no feeling of quixotic restlessness induce her to rashly leave home. It may be her plain duty to remain at home . . . she can pay her way by filling in all the little spaces in home life as only a dear daughter can, by lifting the weight of care from her mother, and by slipping in a soft word or a smile where it is like oil on the troubled waters of a father's spirit. . . . There is no household work such that a girl should deem it beneath her position to know how to do it . . . whether her destiny lies in the old country or the colonies, her knowledge of home matters will be the greatest blessing to herself and others.
>
> (Vol. 1, 1880–81, p. 769)

This early feature shows quite clearly how, throughout the period 1880–1910, the *Girl's Own Paper* seems to have operated in a 'prefigurative' way.[32] That is, it made a bridge between the rapidly changing experience of being young and female in British society and the residual notion of what it *should* be like. New ideas about education, careers for women, health and exercise were made acceptable by being related to traditional values, behaviour, and occupations. (Part and parcel of this change was the gradual recognition that girlhood and womanhood were different states with different needs and interests.) By 1894 the magazine had been redesigned to appeal more specifically to a younger audience.

The new, more modern, mast-head for 1894.

Non-fiction

A survey of the non-fiction features soon shows up the tension between a realistic concern with the lives and futures of women and an ideological loyalty to traditional beliefs about the role of women and the definition of femininity. Thus encouragement and advice for girls about training themselves for work and being prepared to earn their own livings is countered by an equally firm insistence on the primacy of domestic duties and traditional voluntary and charitable work. There *were* pieces which seem positively to celebrate work by encouraging readers to avoid lives of burdensome dependency on male relations and to protect themselves against the vagaries of fate. Single, unsupported women of all ages who managed to maintain themselves were applauded. However, their activities were carefully presented as feminine in the traditional sense. Significantly, these are not radicals in pursuit of equality or desiring to compete with men, but part of an increasing band of females who had to earn their livings but still wished to be considered ladies. The problem of making the two goals compatible was outlined by Sarah Ellis in *The Daughters of England* (1842):

> As society is at present constituted, a lady may do almost anything from motives of charity or zeal. . . . But so soon as woman begins to receive money . . . as soon as she makes money by own efforts . . . she is transformed into a tradeswoman, and she must find her place in society as such. (p. 37)

The *Girl's Own Paper* was concerned with minimising the anxieties generated by new political ideas, developments in education, career structures and increased mobility for young women. It sought to convince its readers that the old values need not be superseded, but could be reconciled with new situations and demands. Girls were not sacrificing their femininity by taking on new tasks and responsibilities, but neither was femininity intrinsically different from what it used to be. Rather, maidenly activity of the right kind could be regarded as training for wifely duties and therefore as preferable to the confined and inactive existences lived by many middle-class girls earlier in the century.

Despite its encouraging girls to work if they had to, the *GOP* joined in the general tendency to marginalise female labour towards the end of the century.[33] The male labour-force feared the expansion of the already considerable reserves of cheap female labour. Working women were accused of making it harder for men to find work, of upsetting the hierarchies of professionalism and, therefore, men's status and even of jeopardising the country's economic stability. Women were discouraged from entering the labour market and directly challenging the supremacy of men. The abandonment of intellectual ambitions or career prospects accordingly came to be associated with patriotic rhetoric, as in L. T. Meade's *A Sweet*

Girl Graduate: when Priscilla Peel opts for the womanly career of governess, she is eulogised in patriotic terms as the type of woman, 'at the root of the true life of a worthy nation'.

The GOP showed girls that they could work without compromising their femininity, by taking on low-status, poorly-paid occupations and continuing in all their usual domestic roles. Again, definitions of middle-class femininity in particular were expanded horizontally, in order to discourage women from becoming burdens on their male relations, but not vertically, with the result that actual power relations were virtually unchanged by this new 'freedom'. The workplace became just another venue in and through which women were shown serving others. Perhaps this attitude was underlined so forcibly because the editor and publishers were male. Whether or not this is the case, it is clear that the GOP was not concerned with providing a platform for the women who were actively engaged in challenging conventional attitudes, but was reacting against change. Neither its fiction nor its features can be interpreted in a subversive way. While there is genuine concern to improve girls' lives, it is not with the goal of challenging male authority. The only political enterprise which can be identified in the paper is the determination to maintain the status quo. It attempts to deflect anxious introspection, particularly in those girls who realised that they would be denied marriage and motherhood, and those who deliberately rejected traditional roles as innately unsatisfying.

In addition to attempting to resolve anxieties arising from the changing role of women, the GOP also dealt with more personal concerns: the state of girls' health, appearance and spirituality. Whereas the BOP discouraged boys from using its pages and services to give vent to private problems and anxieties, its sister paper regularly included features and correspondence which dealt with precisely these matters. There was basic advice on diet and skin care for those concerned with their weight and complexion, and recipes for shampoos and lotions to improve the health and appearance of hair and skin. The paper also saw itself as fulfilling a pastoral function. Many girls wrote about their religious lives and experiences. Only the editor's replies survive, yet it seems safe to conclude from these that often the spiritual crises described were associated with psychic distress.

> A. S. A. G. + E. T. A. E. (A lover of Christ). – You have our sincere sympathy, and with it the expression of our fullest satisfaction in your religious state, and the assurance that you may justly find rest in your Saviour's forgiving love. But your nerves are terribly out of order, and if you persist in this perpetual analysing of your thoughts, and the action of your will in connection with them, your mind will become affected, and melancholy madness will probably be induced. . . . Occupy yourself in some active employment useful to others; work in a garden . . . mix in cheerful society, go to bed early . . . and always have an interesting book to take up when this morbid self-examination comes in. (Vol. 3, 1885–6)

Such 'nervous complaints' were a familiar aspect of late-Victorian and Edwardian femininity and so fitted easily into the pages of the *GOP* (there is no equivalent in the boys' magazine), yet the advice given, as in the above reply, is of the 'no-nonsense' variety which refuses to recognise that the problem has a real basis. Thus the paper simultaneously provided an outlet for anxiety (and some documentation as to the extent of such fears among its readers) but refused to acknowledge it as genuine. The *GOP*'s failure to provide a platform for the discussion of problems relating to the female self and its advice to suppress the desire to challenge and question the nature of their roles and their reactions to them both helped to create the large number of incapacitated female hysterics of this period. Unable to articulate their anxieties and anger, these women found that their bodies were acting for them metonymically. 'Ill', 'invalid', 'unwell', came to stand for what these women were. Because their conditions came about as a result of the need to displace their frustrations, they covertly condemned the society which so effectively silenced and regulated them.

The editor's advice to serve others and forget the self is characteristic of the residual, Ruskinian attitude to women. Reading too had come to be regarded as an acceptable feminine pastime for the leisured classes, provided that what was read was 'appropriate'. While notions of what constituted proper reading for young women varied according to the age, class and sex of the definer, the *Girl's Own Paper*, including its fiction, was considered acceptable by most. It is in its fiction that girl readers were most likely to encounter, not only socially correct definitions of femininity (and masculinity), but also the kind of reading experience which would encourage their acceptance.

Fiction

Fiction occupied a slightly smaller proportion of the *GOP* than it did in the *BOP* – approximately six-and-a-half pages in each sixteen page number. There were generally two serials running consecutively as well as poems and short stories. Because illustrations tended to be generous, each instalment was quite short, which meant that it could take many months for a story to be completed. This combination of factors resulted in the actual fiction content of the magazine being substantially less than in the boys' paper. What there was was invariably moral, but the explicitness of the instruction varied greatly. In some stories it is very near the surface; in others, domestic romance predominates. Though the skill of some of the contributors managed to raise the level above the equivalent in today's girls magazines, the basic elements have remained more or less constant. Girls learned that they are loved and admired not for their beauty but for their behaviour. If they are modest, virtuous, constant and untiring in the service of others, they will win the love and respect of the hero – and find themselves thought beautiful into the bargain. The battles they have to wage to mould themselves into the feminine ideal take place internally and are not acknowledged, though they are rewarded by marriage. The settings are almost invariably domestic, and generally English.

Although there were exceptions, and although among its contributors the *GOP* had some of the best writers for girls of the day, many of whom would have felt the conflicting demands of their professional and female roles, its fiction invariably creates a position for the reader which ultimately sanctions a conventional definition of femininity. The *GOP* was not hostile to improved education for girls and women, but it was concerned with reconciling changes in women's roles with traditional feminine virtues. The overall message was the same for girls of all classes: if you weren't forming a society for maternal welfare or wiping the frowns from paternal brows, you could be 'the sunbeam of the factory', or the angel of the village school.

Thus the *Girl's Own Paper*, despite its concern with female welfare and the reform of legislation and attitudes which victimised women, is ultimately conservative. Its reforming zeal did not extend to wanting to make women more central to the running of society. There is no attempt to include critiques of patriarchy or the relationship between the role of women and capitalism. Rather, it acts essentially as a placebo which disguises a determination not to explore such issues or to encourage readers to seek genuine independence and autonomy.

Conclusion

But there is one thing that's as strange as can be,
Whatever Miss T eats, turns into Miss T!

(Anonymous)

The effects of the seemingly self-evident assumption that boys
need boys' books and girls need girls' books has been the
focus of this study. Why is that thought to be so? For how
long has it been thought? Who decides what shall be a boys'
book, and what a book for girls? Do all boys and girls 'need'
to read books within their own canons? What is the effect on
the crucial acquisition of sexual identity through sex-typed
reading? These are some of the questions which surface as
soon as the 'common sense' behind the division is explored.

In spite of the problems caused by trying to understand the
representation of sexuality (or any other representational
system) in works from which we are historically separated, it
is important to look at juvenile fiction in its own childhood
years for what it can teach us about the texts and images of
childhood produced in our own time. Thus, although I have
been concerned with popular juvenile fiction from the
Victorian/Edwardian eras, my intention has been to understand the relationship between the developments which took
place then and our understanding of today's fiction for young
readers and the part it plays in forming sexual identity.

The work which I have discussed appears to be very
different from today's juvenile fiction, but the difference is
superficial. Walter Benjamin has observed the tendency to
disparage elements from previous periods which seem so

151

outmoded as to be meaningless and alien and which threaten to disappear irretrievably.[1] Yet, as he goes on to say, images of the past do not really disappear in the sense of ceasing to exist. They may be altered, assimilated and eventually become invisible, but just as individual words carry with them all their multiple meanings and usages, so images of the past are contained within images of the present, even though we may not always be aware that this is so. Today's juvenile fiction carries within it images, structures, attitudes and value systems which are at least partially shaped by their earlier counterparts. One obvious reason for this relationship is that the adult writers of contemporary children's fiction were once child readers of fiction written for them and so are in some ways responding to what they experienced. Another is the tendency for young people's reading to be influenced by books from the past. Surveys have regularly found that juvenile reading still tends to have a curiously nineteenth-century flavour. Texts such as *Black Beauty*, *The Secret Garden*, *Little Women*, *What Katy Did*, *Treasure Island*, the 'Alice' books and selected Dickens texts remain staple ingredients in the young reader's literary diet.[2]

Perhaps more important still is the attitude, conveyed in children's fiction itself, that what is read is important. This conviction underpins most books for children and particularly those which are concerned with developing the imagination while maintaining a bourgeois notion of innocent, powerful childhood. Reading is an activity which unites author and reader and establishes shared values. E. Nesbit was particularly fond of classifying characters in terms of what they had read. At the beginning of *The Wouldbegoods* (1901), the following description of Daisy and Denny's aunt makes it clear that she is not enlightened:

No one but that kind of black beady tight lady would say 'little boys'. She is like Miss Murdstone in *David Copperfield*. I should like to tell her so; but she would not understand. I don't suppose she has ever read anything but *Markham's History* and *Mangnall's Questions* – improving books like that.

(from Chapter 1, 'The jungle')

It transpires that Daisy's character, too, has been warped by reading 'the wrong sort of book'; she is cured of her inability to play and socialise properly through doses of books such as *The Count of Monte Cristo*.

The assumption behind this kind of self-referential attitude within children's literature is that as surely as 'you are what you eat', so you are what you read. That is to say, the words young people read and 'inwardly digest' feed their image of themselves and colour their relationship with the world. There are now a number of media which compete with books in offering the child models and languages to use in constructing an image of the self. I do not underestimate their power or value, but reading is still one of the main ways of acquiring language. It has the advantage of being approved of by most adults and institutions – children are actively encouraged to read. However, the relationship between the child and the book is becoming increasingly complex. For instance, publishers now frequently produce printed versions of texts first introduced to the child on the screen. Sometimes this relationship is straight-forward: the cartoon becomes a book or comic. Often, how-ever, books are freely adapted for television or cinema and then reissued in their original form (usually with a cover depicting a scene from the film or programme). Many children have become confused and disgruntled when they discover the difference between Disney's portrayal of, say, *The Jungle Book* and Kipling's original.

Whatever a child's contact with a book – whether it be via the printed page or via the small or large screen – the images and languages it contains affect his/her perception of the world. I have traced the way in which a variety of factors – principally publishers' marketing strategies, educational policies and tradi-tional expectations (including assumptions about what children 'need' and need to know) – converged at the end of the last century, resulting in the manufacture of separate literatures for boys and girls. These separate literatures encouraged adherence to images of masculinity and femininity prevailing in the middle of the last century. In doing so they rejected modifica-tions to attitudes towards sexual difference (and particularly those surrounding the nature of femininity) which were being incorporated in adult fiction. Whereas through the dialectical nature of the relationship between literature and culture adult novels were accustoming the public to changes in the social meanings of masculinity and femininity, both boys' and girls' fiction can instead be seen as conservative examples of what Althusser has identified as literature's unique capacity to reveal (and rupture) dominant contemporary ideologies. In the case of juvenile fiction, rather than making a radical challenge to attitudes which were in the process of becoming dominant, there was an attempt to replace them with images and discourses based on residual meanings within the social definition of the term.[3] I have been concerned to show how and why such attitudes developed in the formative years of juvenile publishing because they continue to affect the whole children's canon today.

Many changes *have* taken place in juvenile fiction over the last decade. Writers are beginning to experiment with form and to broach issues which would previously have been thought unsuitable for young readers (sex, violence, nihilism). The comfortable bourgeois belief in childhood innocence is repeatedly challenged by more realistic accounts of childhood experience and perceptions. In spite of these alterations, there has been little movement in the representation of sexual difference.

The influence of what is read on assumptions about sexual difference has been the concern of educationists for a number of years, and efforts have been made to amend the stereotyping of male and female roles in areas such as fairy tales and school reading books. The efficacy of what are essentially cosmetic changes is questionable as long as they belie the structure of the stories: it is not sufficient to make Cinderella a plumber if winning the prince is still her only goal in life.[4] Moreover, in the kind of fiction which is likely to comprise a young person's private reading, the imaging of masculinity and femininity has altered very little since 1910. Much-loved authors, such as Arthur Ransome, Enid Blyton, and C. S. Lewis, certainly continue in this vein. Girls in their stories may differ from those in stories written fifty years earlier in that they dress differently, are more active and experience more physical freedom, but their roles have remained more or less constant. Popular, low-status girls' books encompassing school, nurse, horse, detective and romantic stories, retain many of the same elements and conventions used by their nineteenth-century equivalents. Tomboys reform and turn into conventional, pretty, conformist and ministering young women. The domestic angel may have been replaced by the cricketer or sky nurse, but ultimately she seeks to please in much the same way as she always did.

Perhaps more surprisingly, in high-quality contemporary juvenile fiction, such as that written by Nina Bawden, Susan Cooper, Alan Garner and Robert Westall, male and female roles are also relatively unchanged. It is usually the girls who provide the link with the past or other cultures and the boys who are armed and carry out the physical battles.

The exception which both proves the rule and suggests that attitudes are being seriously questioned is Gene Kemp's *The Turbulent Term of Tyke Tiler* (1977), in which the protagonist's gender is deliberately, but quite subtly, withheld until the final pages of the book. Tyke's behaviour in class, attitudes towards members of the opposite sex, associates and interests all lead the reader to believe that she is a 'he' on a first reading. There are numerous clues throughout the text that this is not the case, but readers tend to ignore them. What Kemp achieves through this device is the foregrounding of the strength of conventions and expectations towards sex roles and to literary categories. The readership of the book would have been quite different had it been titled *Theodora Tiler's Troublesome Term*.

Kemp's work is a beginning. It highlights the existence of conventions which perpetuate notions of sexual difference originating in the last century. However, the relationship between children's reading and the reproduction of sexual roles needs to be better understood and more fully explored by writers, publishers and purchasers. In her collection of essays, *Women and Other Glorified Outcasts* (1985), Nina Auerbach discusses the need to, 'dissolve the prison of gender by showing men and women sharing a common consciousness within a common culture'.[5] While their reading lives diverge so early, with male reading being steered away from fiction as part of the process of making boys autonomous, and female readers being guided towards fiction of a kind which seems to justify passivity and self-regulation, this commonality is seriously hindered.

Notes

Introduction

1. R. Altick, *The English Common Reader* (Chicago: University of Chicago Press, 1957), p. 231.
2. *ibid.*, p. 233.
3. *ibid.*, p. 232 and p. 308.
4. E. J. Salmon, 'What girls read', *The Nineteenth Century* (October 1886), p. 529.
5. *ibid.*, p. 520.

Chapter 1

1. See, for instance, G. Avery, *Nineteenth-Century Children* (London: Hodder and Stoughton, 1965); J. S. Bratton, *The Impact of Victorian Children's Fiction* (London: Croom Helm, 1981); M. Cadogan and P. Craig, *You're a Brick, Angela!* (London: Victor Gollancz, 1986); N. M. Cutt, *Ministering Angels* (Wormley, Herts: Five Owls Press, 1979); P. Howarth, *Play Up and Play the Game* (London: Eyre Methuen, 1973); C. Meigs, *A Critical History of Children's Literature* (London: Macmillan, 1953); J. Rose, *The Case of Peter Pan or the Impossibility of Children's Literature* (London: Macmillan, 1984); L. Salway (ed.), *A Peculiar Gift* (London: Kestrel Books, 1976); M. F. Thwaite, *From Primer to Pleasure* (London: Library Association, 1963); and N. Tucker (ed.), *Suitable for Children?* (Brighton: Sussex University Press, 1976).
2. J. S. Bratton, *The Impact of Victorian Children's Fiction* (London: Croom Helm, 1984), p. 14.
3. This topic is discussed at length in a great many sources. See particularly J. Ackland, 'Elementary education and the decay of literature', *The Nineteenth Century* (March 1894); Altick (1957); 'The byways of literature: Reading for the million', *Blackwoods Magazine*, vol. LXXIV (August 1858); R. C. Terry, *Victorian Popular Fiction, 1860–1880* (London: Macmillan, 1983), and R.

K. Webb, *The British Working Class Reader, 1790–1848* (London: George Allen & Unwin, 1955).

4. Reward books were given as prizes for scholarship, attendance and merit in schools and Sunday schools. They were produced and distributed on a large scale and, though initially designed to instruct, it was in their manufacture that many commercial and technical innovations were first introduced into juvenile publishing.

5. From the report of the 1832 SPCK standing committee, quoted in B. Alderson, 'Tracts, rewards and fairies: the Victorian contribution to children's literature', *Essays in the History of Publishing in Celebration of the 250th Anniversary of the House of Longman* (ed. A. Briggs, London: Longman, 1974), p. 266.

6. SPCK annual report, 1870–1, p. 13.

7. RTS annual report for 1879 quoted in P. W. Musgrave, *From Brown to Bunter: The life and death of the school story* (London: Routledge & Kegan Paul, 1985), p. 114.

8. Terry (1983), p. 23.

9. Alderson (1974), p. 273.

10. A. Ellis, *A History of Children's Reading and Literature* (London: Pergamon Press, 1969), p. 69.

11. See Ackland (1894); G. S. Chalmers, *Reading Easy* (London: the Broadsheet King, 1976); J. Purvis, 'The experience of schooling for working-class boys and girls in nineteenth-century England', *Defining the Curriculum: Histories and ethnographies* (eds Goodson and Ball, Barcombe: Falmer Press, 1984); L. Stone, 'Literacy and education in England: 1640–1900', *Past and Present*, No. 42 (1969); and Webb (1955).

12. L. James, 'The trouble with Betsy: periodicals and the common reader in mid-nineteenth-century England', *The Victorian Periodical Press: Samplings and soundings* (eds Shattock and Wolff, London: Leicester University Press, 1982), p. 354.

13. 'Byways of literature', pp. 202–3.

14. J. M. Goldstrom, *Education: Elementary education 1780–1900* (Newton Abbot: David & Charles, 1972), p. 29.

15. From Smiles's *The Education of the Working Classes* (1845), quoted in Webb (1955), p. 15.

16. K. Clarke, 'Public and private children: infant education in the 1820s and 1830s', *Language, Gender and Childhood* (eds Steedman, Urwin and Walkerdine, London: Routledge & Kegan Paul, 1985), p. 75.

17. Quoted in Webb (1955), Frontis.

18. Purvis, 'The experience of schooling', p. 107.
19. Goldstrom (1972), p. 98.
20. See Purvis, 'The experience of schooling', and E. E. Rich, *The 1870 Education Act: A study of public opinion* (London: Longman, 1970).
21. Charles Dickens, *Great Expectations* (1860–61), Chapter 7.
22. Purvis, 'The experience of schooling', p. 93.
23. I am grateful to Alan Sinfield for his discussion of the colonial master–servant relationship (1987 graduate colloquia, University of Sussex) which informed this point.
24. Stone, 'Literacy and education', pp. 83–4.
25. Altick (1957) discusses the way in which educational/literacy reforms were designed to strengthen the existing social structure rather than to enrich the intellectual or emotional lives of the work-force, p. 143. Rich (1970) notes that from the outset educational grants were administered according to the dictum that, 'no plan of education ought to be encouraged in which intellectual instruction is not subordinate to the regulation of thoughts and habits of the children', p. 18. These findings are elaborated and supported in J. M. Goldstrom's 'The control of education and the socialisation of the working-class child, 1830–1860,' in *Popular Education and Socialisation in the Nineteenth Century* (ed. P. McCann, London: Methuen, 1977). For a contemporary discussion of the issues see J. P. Mahaffy, 'Modern education', *The Nineteenth Century*, 1897.
26. Stone, 'Literacy and education', p. 72.
27. Purvis, 'The experience of schooling', p. 97.
28. Webb (1955), p. 23.
29. Z. Shavit, *The Poetics of Children's Literature* (Athens (GA): University of Georgia Press, 1986). For a discussion of canonised and uncanonised books, see pp. 33–68.
30. See, for instance, the comments of E. J. Salmon and Mrs Molesworth in L. Salway, *A Peculiar Gift* (London: Kestrel Books, 1976), pp. 334 and 341.
31. Categories described by Cecil Reddie, Headmaster of Abbotsholme School, for the Bryce Commission, quoted in J. Lawson and H. Silver, *A Social History of Education in England* (London: Methuen, 1973), p. 344.
32. S. Ball, 'A subject of privilege: English and the school curriculum 1906–35', ed. Ball, *Curriculum Practice: Some sociological case studies* (Barcombe: Falmer Press, 1983), p. 65.
33. Lawson and Silver (1973), p. 344.

34. Rose, (1984), Chapter 5.
35. Ellis (1969), p. 48.
36. Rose (1984), Chapter 5.
37. *ibid.* Rose's use of words such as 'concrete' and 'synthetic' to describe a particular reading level is derived from educational sources. See S. Humphries, *Hooligans or Rebels? An oral history of working-class childhood and youth 1889–1939* (Oxford: Basil Blackwell, 1981). Humphries notes that as late as 1944 the modification of the tripartite education system claimed to correspond to three clearly defined types of intellect and character, placing at the top those capable of abstract thought, and at the bottom those pupils who could not progress beyond a concrete level, p. 16.
38. Rose (1984), p. 119.
39. See Shavit (1986), especially pp. 33–68; 134.
40. Shavit (1986) suggests that the difference between these two categories is largely dependent on attitudes held by adult readers. She maintains that all children's books are written in the knowledge that adults will be responsible for establishing their literary reputations – only those books which fulfil adult expectations and requirements will be classified as 'good' (p. 68). Such books operate a notion of dual readership, deliberately courting the approval of adults on the basis of subject, content and form. This kind of writing depends for its success on the fact that children and adults will generally respond to texts differently. Adults, whose experience of reading will generally be greater than the young reader's, recognise and value complexity and sophisticated elements of which the child is unaware. The child reader is satisfied with the reduced and simplified material in the text which will comprise the bulk of his/her understanding and enjoyment. According to Shavit, the child reader, for whom the book is ostensibly written, is not intended to realise it fully, pp. 70–7. Dual readership is discussed in more detail in Chapter 4.
41. Rose (1984), p. 120.
42. I use the word 'realism' to describe narrative technique; not content. Realism depends on certain assumptions and a particular kind of relationship between author, narrator and reader. For instance, it is primarily interested in character, offers a centre from which the narrative becomes intelligible, moves through a series of complications to a satisfying resolution, etc. A good

discussion of realism is contained in Belsey's *Critical Practice* (1980). With the possible exception of recreating an illusion of the world as it is commonly perceived (though other equally 'real' worlds are created), children's fiction tends to adhere firmly to the conventions of realism.

43. See A. Bacon, 'English literature becomes a university subject: King's College, London as a pioneer', *Victorian Studies*, Summer 1986.
44. Rose (1984), p. 118.
45. *ibid.*, p. 108.
46. 'The byways of literature', p. 201.
47. Humphries (1981) observes that 'in the late nineteenth century the dramatic growth of juvenile literature, especially the penny-dreadfuls, aroused moral panic among sections of the middle class, which linked these pernicious influences directly with resistance to authority and crimes committed by working-class youth.' p. 6.
48. In *Juvenile Literature as it is* (1888) Salmon provides a number of examples of what he perceives as 'copycat' crimes. He quotes the examples of a son who shot his father and two boys who became burglars after reading their 'weekly packets of poison'.
49. M. Dalziel, *Popular Fiction One Hundred Years Ago* (London: Cohen & West, 1957), p. 45.
50. Salmon (1888), p. 191.
51. *ibid.*
52. *Penny Dreadfuls and Comics: English periodicals for children from Victorian times to the present day* (catalogue of exhibition at the Bethnal Green Museum of Childhood, 2 June–2 October, 1983), p. 22.
53. Purvis, 'The experience of schooling', p. 112.
54. *ibid.* p. 101.
55. *ibid.*, p. 93.
56. *ibid.* p. 107.
57. *ibid.*, p. 108.
58. J. Weeks, *Sex, Politics, and Society: The regulation of sexuality since 1800* (London: Longman, 1981), p. 68.
59. Ball, 'A subject of privilege', p. 76.
60. Musgrave (1985), p. 86 and p. 210.

Chapter 2

1. M. J. Lane and K. A. Furness-Lane, *Books Girls Read; A survey*

of reading habits in a comprehensive school for girls (London: Society of Young Publishers, 1967), p. 25.

2. See Humphries (1981).

3. I. Jan, 'Children's literature and bourgeois society in France since 1860', *Yale French Studies: The Child's Part* (1969), p. 61.

4. A key example of this is Eve Garnett's series based on *The Family from One End Street* (1937), which attempted to give a realistic picture of working-class family life, but never really moved away from middle-class perspectives. As a consequence, the book came to be condemned as patronising. A more recent attempt to break away from the stereotypes and structures imposed by allegiance to middle-class values can be seen in the 'Nippers' series (begun in 1968), edited by Leila Berg.

5. See P. Coveney, *The Image of Childhood* (Harmondsworth: Penguin Books, 1967), p. xi. It is useful to remember that this image was not held throughout the nineteenth century. Nina Auerbach discusses the vicissitudes in attitudes towards children, real and fictional, in *Romantic Imprisonment; Women and other glorified outcasts* (New York: Columbia University Press, 1988).

6. See S. Prickett, *Victorian Fantasy* (Hassocks: Harvester Press, 1979).

7. P. Brooks, 'Towards supreme fictions', *Yale French Studies: The Child's Part* (1969), pp. 10–11. Shavit (1986) expands this point in her discussion of ambivalent texts. She writes, 'the ambivalent text has two implied readers: a pseudo-addressee and a real one. The child, the official reader of the text, is not meant to realise it fully and is much more an excuse for the text rather than its genuine addressee,' p. 71.

8. See Chapter 1, note 40; also, Chapter 5.

9. P. Ariès, 'At the point of origin', *Yale French Studies: The Child's Part* (1969) p. 15.

10. C. Steedman, 'Prisonhouses', *Feminist Review*, 20 (June, 1985), p. 4.

11. E. J. Salmon, 'Should children have a special literature?', in Salway (ed.) (1976), pp. 336–7.

12. *ibid.*

13. C. M. Yonge, *What Books to Lend and What to Give* (London: National Society's Depository, 1888), p. 10.

14. Musgrave (1985), p. 115.

15. Yonge (1888), p. 6.

16. F. Whitehead, *et al.* (eds), *Children and Their Books* (London:

Macmillan Educational, 1977). The findings of the Schools Council research study into children's reading concluded that, 'At all ages, girls read more than boys', p. 273.

17. M. Meek; A. Warlow; G. Barton (eds), *The Cool Web: The pattern of children's reading* (London: Bodley Head, 1977), p. 8.

18. B. Bettelheim, *The Uses of Enchantment: The meaning and importance of fairy tales* (London: Thames and Hudson, 1976), p. 226.

19. N. Tucker (ed.), *Suitable for Children? Controversies in children's literature* (Brighton: Sussex University Press, 1976), p. 266.

20. Bettelheim (1976), p. 5.

21. Belsey (1980), p. 66.

22. N. Chodorow, *The Reproduction of Mothering: Psychoanalysis and the sociology of gender* (Berkeley and Los Angeles: University of California Press, 1978), p. 181.

23. *ibid.*, p. 7. It is also useful to bear in mind the point made by J. Laplanch and J. B. Pontalis in 'Fantasy and the origins of sexuality', in V. Burgin, *et al.* (eds), *Formations of Fantasy* (London: Methuen, 1986), that the child receives its sexual existence from without before being able to distinguish within and without, p. 8.

24. Chodorow (1978), p. 54.

25. *ibid.*, p. 106. See also A. Oakley, *Sex, Gender and Society* (London: Temple Smith, 1972). Oakley also emphasises the influence of reading on the formation of sexual identity, p. 185.

26. Chodorow (1978), p. 181.

27. F. Whitchard, *et al.* (eds), (1977) p. 114.

28. *ibid.*, pp. 212–13.

29. See Altick (1957), pp. 161; 180; 186.

30. See C. L. Peterson, *The Determined Reader* (New Jersey: Rutgers University Press, 1986), especially p. 29. See also N. Holland, *Five Readers Reading* (New Haven: Yale University Press, 1975), p. 18. Holland identifies a terminology of reading based upon images of food and loss of self which indicates that such a state is being sought. Significantly, such descriptions are reserved almost exclusively for the reading of fiction, thus highlighting the difference in reading experiences for boys and girls.

31. B. Benvenuto and R. Kennedy, *The Works of Jacques Lacan: An introduction* (London: Free Association Books, 1986), p. 131.

Notes

32. E. Wright, 'Modern psychoanalytic criticism', *Modern Literary Theory* (eds A. Jefferson and D. Robey, London: Batsford, 1983), p. 129.

Chapter 3

1. J. Ruskin, *Sesame and Lilies* (London: George Allen, 1871), p. 107.
2. *ibid.*, p. 130.
3. Musgrave (1985), pp. 16–17.
4. Salmon (1888), p. 209.
5. S. Heath, *The Sexual Fix* (London: Macmillan, 1982). Discussing the indicators that sexuality was being perceived as problematic during this period Heath writes, 'On the one hand, there is a pressure of the sexual, a problem, an awareness of something that is now difficult and that can only – that must – be understood as medical, contained ideologically and institutionally . . . within medical representations as illness, disorder, disturbance of the individual. Hence the characteristic and extensive medicalisation of the sexual, of sexuality – which thus simultaneously emerges as a word, a notion, to mark the doubting, the problem, the new awareness.' p. 13.
6. Weeks (1981), p. 7.
7. *ibid.*, p. 68.
8. *ibid.*, p. 12.
9. *ibid.*, p. 23.
10. P. Howarth, *Play Up and Play the Game: The heroes of popular fiction* (London: Methuen, 1973), p. 43. R. M. Ballantyne's (1825–94) theory of raising boys epitomises this attitude. While believing that boys should be brought up to take risks so that they could cultivate the cool heads and self-possession needed in maturity, he also suggests that those who 'muffed it' in an emergency did so through lack of training, not through being insufficiently manly. The guilt was on their guardians, not on the boys themselves.
11. Quoted in Musgrave (1985), p. 180.
12. Howarth (1973), p. 37.
13. P. Dunae, 'Boys' literature and the idea of empire, 1870–1914', *Victorian Studies*, Autumn, 1980, p. 106.
14. Howarth (1973), p. 92.
15. Dunae, 'Boys literature', p. 113.

16. Musgrave (1985), p. 34.
17. Howarth (1973), p. 60.
18. Rose (1984), p. 4.
19. 'The whole body of successful boys' literature cannot be more concisely described than as a vast system of hero worship.' Salmon (1888), p. 217.
20. Weeks (1981), p. 84.
21. M. Foucault, *The History of Sexuality*, vol. I, trans. R. Hurley (London: Allen Lane, 1979), p. 30.
22. F. Whitehead, *et al.* (eds) (1977), p. 114.

Chapter 4

1. 'Wherever English is spoken one imagines that Mr. Henty's name is known. One cannot enter a schoolroom or look at a boy's bookshelf without seeing half-a-dozen of his familiar volumes', *Review of Reviews*, 1982, quoted in G. Arnold, *Held Fast for England: G. A. Henty, imperialist boys' writer* (London: Hamish Hamilton, 1980), p. 25. *The Oxford Companion to Children's Literature* quotes *The Times* as saying, 'he understands boys' tastes better than any man living', and credits him with having been 'most boys' main source of historical knowledge'.
2. The principal biographies of each are: *George Alfred Henty: The story of an active life* by G. Manville Fenn (1907) and *Talbot Baines Reed: Author, bibliographer, typefounder* by S. Morrison (1960). Other books and articles are referred to throughout the chapter and in the bibliography.
3. R. A. Huttenback, 'G. A. Henty and the vision of empire', *Encounter*, vol. 35 (1970), p. 53.
4. S. L. Gilman, *Difference and Pathology: Stereotypes of sexuality, race, and madness* (New York: Cornell University Press, 1985), p. 20.
5. *ibid.* See also p. 240.
6. *ibid.*, p. 19.
7. See 'Female sexuality in *fin-de-siècle* Vienna' in Gilman (1985).
8. Howarth (1973), p. 80.
9. A. P. Thornton, 'G. A. Henty's British Empire', *Fortnightly Review*, vol. 175 (1954), p. 101.
10. Howarth (1973), p. 77.
11. *ibid.*
12. Thornton (1954), p. 97.

13. M. Naidis, 'G. A. Henty's idea of India', *Victorian Studies*, vol. 8 (1964), p. 50. By Naidis's calculations, at least eighty of Henty's works were historical novels for juveniles. Henty's work was translated into French, Danish, Norwegian and Spanish. By 1898 one of Henty's publishers claimed that he had a circulation of between 150,000–250,000 copies a year.
14. Huttenback (1970), pp. 46–7.
15. E. Showalter, *The Female Malady: Women, madness and English culture, 1830–1980* (London: Pantheon Books, 1985), p. 117.
16. J. S. Bratton explored these pressures in a paper given at the third conference on children's literature (Bulmershe, 1987).
17. P. Dunae, '*Boy's Own Paper*: origins and editorial policies', *The Private Library*, vol. 9, series 2 (Winter, 1976), p. 127.
18. Musgrave (1985), p. 115.
19. Jack Cox, *Take a Cold Tub, Sir! The story of the Boy's Own Paper* (Guildford: Lutterworth Press, 1982), p. 13.
20. *ibid.*, p. 10.
21. *ibid.*
22 Salmon (1888), pp. 17–18.
23. J. A. Mangan, 'The grit of our forefathers: invented traditions, propaganda and imperialism', in J. M. MacKenzie (ed.), *Imperialism and Popular Culture* (Manchester: Manchester University Press, 1986), p. 129.

Chapter 5

1. This debate filled the pages of parents' magazines, religious, educational and medical journals, and pieces were directed at girl readers themselves. See, for instance: Mrs. Ellis, *The Daughters of England* (1842); John Gregory, *A Father's Legacy to his Daughters* (1786); Emily Davies, *The Higher Education of Women* (1866), all of which were in circulation at this time. A number of examples are also provided in recent studies such as J. N. Burstyn's *Victorian Education and the Ideal of Womanhood* (London: Croom Helm, 1980), and E. O. Hellerstein *et al.* (eds), *Victorian Women: A documentary account* (Stanford: Stanford University Press, 1981).
2. Yonge (1888), p. 10.
3. See Chapter 5, note 1.
4. G. Avery, *Nineteenth-Century Children: Heroes and heroines in English children's stories 1780–1900* (London: Hodder and Stoughton, 1965), p. 149.

5. S. M. Gilbert and S. Gubar, *The Madwoman in the Attic: The woman writer and the nineteenth-century literary imagination* (London: Yale University Press, 1979), p. 57.

6. Bettleheim (1976), p. 25.

7. See Patricia Thomson, *The Victorian Heroine: a changing ideal 1837–1873* (London: Oxford University Press, 1956).

8. Rose (1984), p. 63; Shavit (1986), p. 63.

9. I use Thomson's (1956) identification of 1837 as the first appearance of revisions to images of femininity in the novel.

10. See Croser and Croser, 'The principal of legitimacy and its patterned infringement in social revolutions' in R. L. Croser (ed.), *The Family: Its structures and functions* (New York: St Martin's Press, 1973), p. 106.

11. D. Gorham, *The Victorian Girl and the Feminine Ideal* (London: Croom Helm, 1982), p. 108.

12. See B. Fowler, 'True to me always: an analysis of women's magazine fiction', in C. Pawling (ed.), *Popular Fiction and Social Change* (London: Macmillan, 1984); T. Modleski, *Loving with a Vengeance: Mass-produced fantasies for women* (London: Methuen, 1982); and V. Walkerdine, 'Some day my prince will come: young girls and the preparation for adolescent sexuality', in A. McRobbie and M. Nava (eds), *Gender and Generation* (London: Macmillan, 1984).

13. G. Eliot, 'Silly novels by lady novelists', *Westminster Review*, vol. LXVI (October, 1856), p. 442.

14. See Heath (1982); Modleski (1982); Pawling (1984) and J. A. Radway, *Reading the Romance* (London: University of North Carolina Press, 1984).

15. See Ball (1983); Salmon (1888) and Yonge (1888). L. Salway (1976) also provides a number of extracts which illustrate this point.

16. Altick (1957), p. 177.

17. Musgrave (1985), p. 63.

18. Rose (1984), p. 84.

19. Salmon, 'What Girls Read', p. 523.

20. See Shavit (1986) for full discussion of 'ambivalent' and 'univalent' texts.

21. Salmon 'What Girls Read', p. 523.

22. Shavit (1986), p. 63.

23. I am indebted to the late Allon White for his lectures on Bakhtin; part of the Modern European Mind lecture series at Sussex University, 1984.

24. See R. Hoggart, *The Uses of Literacy: Aspects of working-class life with special reference to publications and entertainments* (Harmondsworth: Penguin Books, 1965), p. 197; and S. Marcus, *The Other Victorians* (London: Meridian, 1977), p. 108.
25. See Chapter 1 of Prickett (1979).

Chapter 6

1. My attention was drawn to this quotation by Sally Mitchell's article, 'Sentiment and suffering: women's recreational reading in the 1860s', *Victorian Studies* (Autumn, 1977), p. 29.
2. E. Abel (ed.), *Writing and Sexual Difference* (Brighton: Harvester, 1982) is largely concerned with this issue.
3. G. Frith, 'The time of your life: the meaning of the school story', in C. Steedman, C. Urwin and V. Walkerdine (eds), *Language, Gender, and Childhood* (London: Routledge & Kegan Paul, 1985), p. 128.
4. E. Everett-Green, 'When I was a girl: reminiscences of girlhood by Evelyn Everett-Green', *The Silver Link* (January 1894).
5. *ibid.*, p. 3.
6. *ibid.*
7. *The Times* (29 April 1932), p. 9.
8. Mitchell, 'Sentiment and suffering', p. 32.
9. *ibid.*, p. 34.
10. I use the phrase 'real relations' in the manner adopted by Catherine Belsey in *Critical Practice* (London: Methuen, 1980). Belsey distinguishes between the 'common sense' approach to culture which accepts as natural attitudes and values which are actually social (i.e. ideologically informed) and an enhanced awareness of the ways in which ideology works which comes closer to understanding the nature of social, and specifically material, relationships. The discussion of the relationship between literature and ideology which Belsey develops (particularly in Chapter 3: 'Addressing the subject') has been useful for me throughout the preparation of this book.
11. J. P. Tompkins, 'Sentimental power: *Uncle Tom's Cabin* and the politics of literary history', *Glyph*, vol. 8 (1981), p. 80.
12. *ibid.*
13. See Tompkins (1981).
14. Cora Kaplan, *Sea Changes: Essays on culture and feminism*

Notes

(London: Verso, 1986), concludes that in the nineteenth century, 'women's fiction and poetry is a site where women actively structured the meaning of sexual difference in society,' p. 3. This belief is also behind the work of Elaine Showalter and the combined studies of Sandra Gilbert and Susan Gubar.

15. Weeks (1981), p. 32.
16. *ibid.*, p. 63.
17. *ibid.*
18. See, for instance, G. L. Fox, ' "Nice girl": social control of women through a value construct', *Signs*, vol. 2, No. 4 (Summer, 1977), pp. 805–817.
19. E. O. Hellerstein *et al.* (eds) (1981), pp. 90–2.
20. *ibid.*, p. 93.
21. Quoted in Forrester (1980), Frontis.
22. C. Hall, 'Private persons versus public someones: class, gender and politics in England, 1780–1850', eds Steedmen *et al.*, *Language, Gender and Childhood* (1985), p. 12.
23. Quoted in Kaplan (1986), p. 154.
24. See Walkerdine, 'Some day my prince will come'.
25. H. Carpenter and M. Prichard (1984), p. 207.
26. M. Cadogan and P. Craig (1986), p. 74.
27. Salmon, 'What Girls Read', p. 520.
28. Quoted in Forrester (1980), p. 520.
29. Walkerdine, 'Some day my prince will come', p. 210.
30. *ibid.*
31. Quoted in Cadogan and Craig (1986), p. 77.
32. Musgrave (1985), p. 8.
33. See Weeks (1981), pp. 65–70.

Conclusion

1. Quoted in Gilman (1985), p. 234.
2. Whitehead *et al.* (eds) (1977), p. 10.
3. Musgrave (1985) discusses Althusser's theories in relation to the school story, pp. 251–2.
4. Walkerdine, 'Some day my prince will come', p. 164.
5. Auerbach (1985), p. xiv.

Bibliography

Books

Abel, E., (ed.) *Writing and Sexual Difference* (Brighton: Harvester, 1982).

Adams, J., *The Conspiracy of the Text; The place of narrative in the development of thought* (London: Routledge & Kegan Paul, 1986).

Allen, W. O. B. and McClure, E., *Two Hundred Years: The history of the Society for Promoting Christian Knowledge 1800–1900* (Chicago: University of Chicago Press, 1957).

Archer, J. and Lloyd, B., *Sex and Gender* (Harmondsworth: Penguin Books, 1982).

Ariès, P., *Centuries of Childhood*, trans. R. Baldick (London: Jonathan Cape, 1962).

Arnold, G., *Held Fast for England: G. A. Henty, imperialist boys' writer* (London: Hamish Hamilton, 1980).

Auerbach, N., *Romantic Imprisonment: Women and other glorified outcasts* (New York: Columbia University Press, 1985).

Avery, G., *Nineteenth-Century Children: Heroes and heroines in English children's stories 1780–1900* (London: Hodder & Stoughton, 1965).

Bakhtin, M. M., *The Dialogic Imagination*, ed. M. Holquist; trans. C. Emerson and M. Holquist (Austin: University of Texas Press, 1981).

Ball, S. J. (ed.), *Curriculum Practice: Some sociological case studies* (Barcombe: Falmer Press, 1983).

Bell, S. G. and Offen, K. M. (eds.), *Women, the Family, and Freedom: The debate in documents*, vol. 2, 1880–1950 (Stanford: Stanford University Press, 1983).

Benevenuto, B. and Kennedy, R., *The Works of Jacques Lacan: An introduction* (London: Free Association Books, 1986).

Bettelheim, B., *The Uses of Enchantment: The meaning and importance of fairy tales* (London: Thames & Hudson, 1976).

Bratton, J. S., *The Impact of Victorian Children's Fiction* (London: Croom Helm, 1981).

Briggs, A. (ed.), *Essays in the History of Publishing in Celebration of the 250th Anniversary of the House of Longman* (London: Longman, 1974).

Burgin, V., Donald, J. and Kaplan, C. (eds), *Formations of Fantasy* (London: Methuen, 1986).

Burstyn, J. N., *Victorian Education and the Ideal of Womanhood* (London: Croom Helm, 1980).

Cadogan, M. and Craig, P., *You're a Brick, Angela! The girls' story 1839–1985* (London: Victor Gollancz, 1986).

Carpenter, H. and Prichard, M., *The Oxford Companion to Children's Literature* (London: Oxford University Press, 1984).

Carpenter, H., *Secret Gardens: A study of the golden age of children's literature* (London: George Allen & Unwin, 1985).

Chalmers, G. S., *Reading Easy 1800–1850: A study of the teaching of reading* (London: The Broadsheet King, 1976).

Chambers, A., *Introducing Books to Children*, 2nd edn (London: Heinemann Educational, 1973).

Chodorow, N., *The Reproduction of Mothering: Psychoanalysis and the sociology of gender* (Berkeley and Los Angeles: University of California Press, 1978).

Cohan, S., *Violation and Repair in the English Novel: The paradigm of experience from Richardson to Woolf* (Detroit: Wayne State University Press, 1986).

Coveney P., *The Image of Childhood* (Harmondsworth: Penguin Books, 1967).

Cox, J., *Take a Cold Tub, Sir! The story of the Boy's Own Paper* (Guildford: Lutterworth Press, 1982).

Crow, D., *The Victorian Woman* (London: George Allen & Unwin, 1971).

Cruse, A., *The Englishman and His Books in the Early Nineteenth Century* (London: George G. Harrap, 1930).

Cruse, A., *The Victorians and Their Books* (London: George Allen & Unwin, 1935).

Cutt, M. N., *Ministering Angels: A study of nineteenth-century evangelical writing for children* (Wormley, Herts: Five Owls Press, 1979).

Dalziel, M., *Popular Fiction One Hundred Years Ago: An unexplored tract of literary history* (London: Cohen & West, 1957).

Dixon, B., *Catching Them Young! Sex, race and class in children's fiction* (London: Pluto Press, 1977).

Dyhouse, C., *Girls Growing Up in Late Victorian and Edwardian England* (London: Routledge & Kegan Paul, 1981).

Ellis, A., *Books in Victorian Elementary Schools* (The Library Association, 1971).

Ellis, A., *A History of Children's Reading and Literature* (London: Pergamon Press, 1969).

Fisher, M., *The Bright Face of Danger* (London: Hodder & Stoughton, 1986).

Forrester, W., *Great Grandmama's Weekly: A celebration of the Girl's Own Paper 1880–1901* (Guildford: Lutterworth Press, 1980).

Foucault, M., *The History of Sexuality*, vol. 1, trans. R. Hurley (London: Allen Lane, 1979).

Freud, S., *On Sexuality: Three essays on the theory of sexuality and other works*, vol. 7, Pelican Freud Library, ed. A. Richards, trans. J. Strachey (Harmondsworth: Penguin Books, 1977).

Fuller, M., *Woman in the Nineteenth Century*, intro. B. Rosenthal (New York: The Norton Library, 1971).

Gifford, D., *Victorian Comics* (London: George Allen & Unwin, 1976).

Gilbert, S. M. and Gubar, S., *The Madwoman in the Attic: The woman writer and the nineteenth-century literary imagination* (London: Yale University Press, 1979).

Gilman, S. L., *Difference and Pathology: Stereotypes of sexuality, race and madness* (New York: Cornell University Press, 1985).

Goldstrom, J. M., *Education: Elementary education 1780–1900* (Newton Abbot: David & Charles, 1972).

Goodson, I. and Ball, S. J. (eds), *Defining the Curriculum: Histories and ethnographies* (Barcombe: Falmer Press, 1984).

Gorham, D., *The Victorian Girl and the Feminine Ideal* (London: Croom Helm, 1982).

Heath, S., *The Sexual Fix* (London: Macmillan, 1982).

Hellerstein, E. O., Hume, L. P. and Offen, K. M. (eds), *Victorian Woman: A documentary account of women's lives in nineteenth-century England, France and the United States* (Stanford: Stanford University Press, 1981).

Hoggart, R., *The Uses of Literacy: Aspects of working-class life with special reference to publications and entertainments* (Harmondsworth: Penguin Books, 1965).

Holland, N. N., *Five Readers Reading* (New Haven: Yale University Press, 1975).

Hope, A. R., *A Book About Boys*, 2nd edn (Edinburgh: William P. Nimmo, 1868).

Howarth, P., *Play Up and Play the Game: The heroes of popular fiction* (London: Eyre Methuen, 1973).

Bibliography

Humphries, S., *Hooligans or Rebels? An oral history of working-class childhood and youth 1889–1939* (Oxford: Basil Blackwell, 1981).

Jan, I., *On Children's Literature*, ed. C. Storr (London: Allen Lane, 1969).

Jefferson, A. and Robey, D., *Modern Literary Theory: A comparative introduction* (London: Batsford, 1983).

Kaplan, C., *Sea Changes: Essays on culture and feminism* (London: Verso, 1986).

Kessler, S. J. and McKenna, W., *Gender: An ethnomethodological approach* (New York: John Wiley & Sons, 1978).

Lacan, J., *Ecrits*, a selection trans. A. Sheridan (London: Tavistock, 1977).

Lane, M. J. and Furness-Lane, K. A., *Books Girls Read: A survey of reading habits carried out in a comprehensive school for girls* (London: Society of Young Publishers, 1967).

Lawson, J. and Silver H., *A Social History of Education in England* (London: Methuen, 1973).

Leeson, R. (ed.), *Children's Books and Class Society Past and Present* (London: Children's Rights Workshop, 1977).

MacKenzie, J. M. (ed.), *Imperialism and Popular Culture* (London: Manchester University Press, 1986).

Manville Fenn, G., *George Alfred Henty: The story of an active life* (London: Blackie & Son, 1907).

Marcus, S., *The Other Victorians: A study of sexuality and pornography in mid-nineteenth century England* (London: Methuen, 1977).

McRobbie, A. and Nava, M. (eds), *Gender and Generation* (London: Macmillan, 1984).

Meek, M., Warlow, A. and Barton, G. (eds), *The Cool Web: The pattern of children's reading* (London: Bodley Head, 1977).

Meigs, C. (ed.), *A Critical History of Children's Literature: A survey of children's books in English from earliest times to the present* (London: Macmillan, 1953).

Mitchell, J. and Rose, J. (eds), *Feminine Sexuality: Jacques Lacan and the Ecole Freudienne*, trans. J. Rose (London: Macmillan, 1982).

Mitchell, S., *The Fallen Angel: Chastity, class and women's reading, 1835–1880* (Bowling Green: Bowling Green University Press, 1981).

Modleski, T., *Loving with a Vengeance: Mass-produced fantasies for women* (London: Methuen, 1982).

Moi, T., *Sexual/Textual Politics: Feminist literary theory* (London: Methuen, 1985).

Bibliography

Morrison, S., *Talbot Baines Reed: Author, bibliographer, typefounder* (London: Cambridge University Press, 1960).

Musgrave, P. W., *From Brown to Bunter: The life and death of the school story* (London: Routledge & Kegan Paul, 1985).

Newton, J. L., Ryan, M. P. and Walkowitz, J. R. (eds), *Sex and Class in Women's History* (London: Routledge & Kegan Paul, 1983).

Oakley, A., *Sex, Gender and Society* (London: Temple Smith, 1972).

Pawling, C. (ed.), *Popular Fiction and Social Change* (London: Macmillian, 1984).

Penny Dreadfuls and Comics: English periodicals for children from Victorian times to the present day, catalogue of exhibition at Bethnal Green Museum of Childhood, 2 June–2 October, 1983 (London: Victoria & Albert Museum, 1983).

Peterson, C. L., *The Determined Reader: Gender and culture in the novel from Napoleon to Victoria* (New Jersey: Rutgers University Press, 1986).

Pinchbeck, I. and Hewitt, M., *Children in English Society*, vol. 2 (London: Routledge & Kegan Paul, 1978).

Prickett, S., *Victorian Fantasy* (Hassocks: Harvester, 1979).

Quigly, I., *The Heirs of Tom Brown* (London: Chatto & Windus, 1982).

Radway, J. A., *Reading the Romance* (London: University of North Carolina Press, 1984).

Rich, E. E., *The Education Act 1870: A study of public opinion* (London: Longman, 1970).

Rose, J., *The Case of Peter Pan or the Impossibility of Children's Fiction* (London: Macmillan, 1984).

Rosenthal, L. M., 'The child informed: attitudes towards the socialization of the child in nineteenth-century English children's literature', unpublished PhD thesis from Columbia University, New York, 1974.

Ruskin, J., *Sesame and Lilies* (London: George Allen, 1904).

Salmon, E. J., *Juvenile Literature as it is* (London: Henry J. Darne, 1888).

Salway, L. (ed.), *A Peculiar Gift: Nineteenth-century writings on books for children* (London: Kestrel Books, 1976).

Schaffer, H. R., *The Origins of Human Social Relations* (London: Academic Press, 1971).

Shattock, J. and Wolff, M. (eds), *The Victorian Periodical Press: Samplings and soundings* (London: Leicester University Press, 1982).

Bibliography

Shavit, Z., *The Poetics of Children's Literature* (Athens, GA: University of Georgia Press, 1986).

Showalter, E., *The Female Malady: Women, madness and English culture 1830–1980* (New York: Pantheon Books, 1985).

Showalter, E., *A Literature of their Own: British Women novelists from Brontë to Lessing* (London: Virago, 1977).

Skura, M., *The Literary Use of the Psychoanalytic Process* (London: Yale University Press, 1981).

Society for Promoting Christian Knowledge, Annual Reports, 1870–1910 (London: SPCK).

Steedman, C., Urwin, C. and Walkerdine, V., *Language, Gender and Childhood* (London: Routledge & Kegan Paul, 1985).

Terry, R. C., *Victorian Popular Fiction, 1860–1880* (London: Macmillan, 1983).

Thomson, P. *The Victorian Heroine: A changing ideal 1837–1873* (London: Oxford University Press, 1956).

Thwaite, M. F., *From Primer to Pleasure: An introduction to the history of children's books in England from the invention of printing to 1900* (London: Library Association, 1963).

Todd, J. (ed.), *Gender and Literary Voice* (London: Holmes & Meier Publishers, 1984).

Tucker, N., *The Child and the Book: A psychological and literary exploration* (Cambridge: Cambridge University Press, 1981).

Tucker, N. (ed.), *Suitable for Children? Controversies in children's literature* (Brighton: Sussex University Press, 1976).

Turner, E. S., *Boys will be Boys: The story of Sweeney Todd, Deadwood Dick, Sexton Blake, Billy Bunter, Dick Barton, et al.* (London: Michael Joseph, 1955).

Thal, H. Van, *Eliza Lynn Linton: The girl of the period* (London: George Allen & Unwin, 1979).

Vicinus, M. (ed.), *Suffer and be Still: Women in the Victorian age* (London: Methuen, 1972).

Webb, R. K., *The British Working-Class Reader 1790–1848: Literacy and social tension* (London: George Allen & Unwin, 1955).

Weeks, J., *Sex, Politics and Society: The regulation of sexuality since 1800* (London: Longman, 1981).

Whitehead, F., Capey, A. C., Maddren, W. and Wellings, A. (eds), *Children and Their Books: The final report of the Schools' Council research project on children's reading habits, 10–15* (London: Macmillan Educational, 1977).

Bibliography

Winnicott, D. W., *Playing and Reality* (London: Tavistock Publications, 1971).

Yonge, C. M., *What Books to Lend and What to Give* (London: National Society's Depository, 1888).

Yonge, C. M., *Womankind* (London: Walter Smith, 1881).

Zipes, J., *Fairy Tales and the Art of Subversion* (London: Heinemann, 1983).

Journal articles, etc.

Ackland, J., 'The decay of literature', *The Nineteenth Century* (March, 1894), pp. 412–23.

Adams, P., 'Feminine sexuality: interview with Juliet Mitchell and Jacqueline Rose', *MF*, vol. 8 (1983), pp. 3–16.

Ariès, P., 'At the point of origin', P. Brooks (ed.), *Yale French Studies: The Child's Part* (1969).

Brook, P., 'Towards supreme fictions', P. Brook (ed.), *Yale French Studies: The Child's Part* (1969).

'Byways of literature: reading for the million' (unsigned), *Blackwoods Magazine*, vol. LXXXIV (August, 1858), pp. 200–16.

Bacon, A., 'English literature becomes a university subject: King's College London, as pioneer', *Victorian Studies* (Summer, 1986), pp. 591–612.

'Boy, only Boy' (unsigned), *The Academy*, vol. 57 (October 1899), pp. 457–8.

Dunae, P., 'Boys' literature and the idea of empire', *Victorian Studies* (Autumn, 1980), pp. 105–21.

Dunae, P., '*Boy's Own Paper*: origins and editorial policies', *The Private Library*, vol. 9, series 2, pt 4 (Winter, 1976), pp. 123–58.

Elliott, G. H., 'Our readers and what they read', *The Library*, vol. VII (1895), pp. 276–81.

Fox, G. L., '"Nice girl": social control of women through a value construct', *Signs*, vol. 2, No. 4 (Summer 1977), pp. 805–17.

Harrington, H. R., 'Childhood and the Victorian ideal of manliness in *Tom Brown's Schooldays*', *The Victorian Newsletter* (Fall, 1973), pp. 13–17.

'Hints on reading: what to read – what to read cautiously – what to leave unread' (unsigned), *The Monthly Packet of Evening Readings for Younger Members of the English Church*, vol. XV (March, 1852), pp. 236–40.

Huttenback, R. A., 'G. A. Henty and the vision of empire', *Encounter*, vol. 35 (1970), pp. 46–53.

Jan, I., 'Children's literature and bourgeois society in France since 1860', P. Brook (ed.), *Yale French Studies: The Child's Part* (1969).

Mahaffy, J. P., 'Modern education', *Nineteenth Century* (1897), pp. 703–15.

Mitchell, S., 'Sentiment and suffering: women's recreational reading in the 1860s', *Victorian Studies* (Autumn, 1977), pp. 29–45.

Naidis, M., 'G. A. Henty's idea of India', *Victorian Studies*, vol. 8 (September, 1964), pp. 49–58.

Salmon, E. J., 'What girls read', *The Nineteenth Century* (October, 1886), pp. 515–29.

Steedman, C., 'Prisonhouses', *Feminist Review* (20 June, 1985), pp. 7–19.

Stone, L., 'Literacy and education in England 1640–1900', *Past and Present*, No. 42 (1969), pp. 69–139.

Thornton, A. P., 'G. A. Henty's British Empire', *Fortnightly Review*, vol. 175 (1954), pp. 97–101.

Tompkins, J. P., 'Sentimental power: *Uncle Tom's Cabin* and the politics of literary history', *Glyph*, vol. 8 (1981), pp. 79–102.

Turnbaugh, R., 'Images of empire: George Alfred Henty and John Buchan', *Journal of Popular Culture*, vol. 9 (1975), pp. 734–41.

Yonge, C. M., 'Children's literature of the last century', I, II and III, *Macmillans Magazine*, Vol. XXX, No. 117 (1869), pp. 229–37, 302–10 and 448–56.

Nineteenth-century juvenile books and periodicals

BOOKS

Because the individual authors each wrote prodigious numbers of books, I have listed only those works cited in the text and not every book read and used indirectly. It has also been impossible to locate the date of each edition used, as publishing practice was not standardized to include this information until after the period concerned.

Coolidge, S., *What Katy Did* (London: Weidenfeld & Nicholson, 1958).

Green, E. E., *Dickie and Dorrie at School* (London: Wells Gardner, Darton, and Co.).

Bibliography

Green, E. E., *Gladys and Gwenyth: The story of a mistake* (London: Thomas Nelson & Sons).

Green, E. E., *Maud Melville's Marriage* (London: Thomas Nelson & Sons, 1899).

Green, E. E., *A Wilful Maid* (London: S. W. Partridge).

Henty, G. A., *Facing Death: Or the hero of the Vaughn Pit – a tale of the coal mines* (London: 1882).

Henty, G. A., *Held Fast for England: A tale of the siege of Gibraltar* (London: 1892).

Henty, G. A., *Jack Archer: A tale of the Crimea* (London: 1883).

Henty, G. A., *One of the 28th: A tale of Waterloo* (London: 1890).

Henty, G. A., *A Soldier's Daughter and Other Stories* (London: Blackie & Son, 1906).

Henty, G. A., *With Clive in India: Or, the beginnings of an empire* (London: Blackie & Son, 1884).

Kipling, R., *Stalky & Co.* (London: Macmillan, 1922).

Meade, L. T., *Girls New and Old* (London: W. R. Chambers, 1896).

Meade, L. T., *Polly: A new-fashioned girl* (London: Cassell & Co., 1911).

Meade, L. T., *A Sister of the Red Cross* (London: Cassell & Co., 1901).

Meade, L. T., *A Sweet Girl Graduate* (London: Cassell & Co., 1897).

Reed, T. B., *The Adventures of a Three-Guinea Watch* (serialised in the *Boy's Own Paper*, 1880).

Reed, T. B., *A Dog With a Bad Name* (London: Religious Tract Society, 1886).

Reed, T. B., *The Fifth Form at St. Dominic's* (serialised in the *Boy's Own Paper*, 1881).

Reed, T. B., *Tom, Dick and Harry* (London: Religious Tract Society, 1892).

PERIODICALS

Atalanta
Boy's Own Paper
Girl's Own Paper
The Silver Link

Index

Index